THE BUSCH-REISINGER MUSEUM

History and Holdings

Compiled by Peter Nisbet and Emilie Norris

Harvard University Art Museums
Cambridge, Massachusetts
1991

This publication has been made possible by the European Friends of the Busch-Reisinger Museum.

Designed by Eleanor Bradshaw, printed by Nimrod Press, edited and produced by Evelyn Rosenthal, project editor, with production supervision by Peter L. Walsh, director of publications and information, Harvard University Art Museums.

ISBN 0-916724-79-4

Contents

DIRECTOR'S FOREWORD

This book admirably documents and narrates the complex history of the Busch–Reisinger Museum and its formative role in the development of art history and of the art museums at Harvard University. Moreover, it is appropriate that the book's publication coincides with the opening of the Busch-Reisinger's new home in Werner Otto Hall, since both book and building were designed to enhance student and scholarly use and awareness of Harvard's rich resources for the study of Central and Northern European works of art. We are enormously grateful to the European Friends of the Busch-Reisinger Museum for having made this publication possible.

While the Busch–Reisinger Museum was founded as the Germanic Museum by Kuno Francke in 1901, one can trace its origins back further still to the early years of the nineteenth century and the appointment of Joseph Buckminster to the Harvard faculty. Buckminster was intent on training young Harvard men in the most current German biblical scholarship, and encouraged George Bancroft and George Ticknor to study further at Göttingen. Soon other students followed and, like Bancroft and Ticknor before them, were transformed by their experience. By the 1830s all of intellectual New England was deeply influenced by Germanic thought. Ralph Waldo Emerson and Margaret Fuller wrote and lectured about German literature and translated Goethe and Eckermann. Henry Wadsworth Longfellow was appointed to succeed George Ticknor at Harvard and gave his inaugural lectures on German and Northern literature. Henry David Thoreau, who was among Longfellow's students at Harvard, dedicated much of his senior year to reading Mme. de Stael and translating Goethe's *Italian Journey*. By mid-century, Harvard's curriculum was deeply influenced by German scholarship. One's basic education was thought to be incomplete if one had not read Kant, Herder, Hegel, and Goethe.

Thus in 1897, when Kuno Francke and two colleagues in the Department of Germanic Languages and Literatures co-authored an article entitled "The Need of a Germanic Museum at Harvard," they were drawing upon the University's century-long commitment to the study of Germanic art, thought, and culture.

The Busch-Reisinger Museum has come a very long way in the nearly one hundred years since its founding. Its collections are far richer, its facilities far better, and its resources far greater. Yet its purpose is the same: to stimulate a broad and deep understanding of German, Central, and Northern European art and culture. That it does so now as part of the Harvard University Art Museums, together with the Fogg Art Museum and the Arthur M. Sackler Museum, only strengthens its mission and further assures its success.

Contributing significantly to this mission and to the cultural and intellectual life of Harvard University and the art-appreciating public are the facilities of Werner Otto Hall, designed for and dedicated to the study and presentation of the Busch-Reisinger Museum's collections. The building, which also includes new quarters for Harvard's Fine Arts Library, represents the generosity of numerous individuals, foundations, and corporations in Europe and America.

One person, however, deserves our special thanks. Werner Otto, founder of Otto Versand and the Werner Otto Foundation, understood the need for new facilities for the Busch-Reisinger Museum and also understood the value of the museum's scholarly mission. Thus it is most fitting that we acknowledge by this publication Dr. Otto's extraordinary gift, the most recent and most glorious contribution to the study of Germanic culture at Harvard in the two centuries since such studies first entered the life of the University.

James Cuno
Elizabeth and John Moors Cabot Director
Harvard University Art Museums

PREFACE

The Busch-Reisinger Museum has, throughout its complicated history, always been as much an idea as anything else. Simply put, it has always existed to promote in every appropriate way the informed enjoyment and critical study of the arts of the German-speaking and related cultures of Central and Northern Europe. This it does today as part of the Harvard University Art Museums, with all that implies for the role of an academic museum, devoted to teaching and research, and belonging to one of the world's great universities. However, the Busch-Reisinger's simple idea has taken concrete form in specific circumstances, adapting itself to the needs and opportunities of changing times. Indeed, the museum has, over nine decades, probably been through more changes of name, building, ambition, and "feel" than any other of comparable importance.

The Busch-Reisinger Museum: History and Holdings is intended to give readers the best possible notion of what to expect from the museum. In a way, this book resembles the extended curriculum vitae or professional résumé of an individual. Divided into several sections, each with different kinds of information reflecting different facets of the museum's past and potential, it introduces the reader to the tasks the museum has adopted over the preceding ninety years, the personalities who decisively influenced its identity, the three buildings in which its evolving missions have been carried out, and the character of the collections that have been shaped by this rich past. By perusing this institutional c.v. (which has the added advantage of being richly illustrated), readers can decide what the museum has to offer that coincides with their particular interests.

It is our hope that this book may stimulate greater use of the museum by the people it exists to serve. It should always be borne in mind, however, that the Busch-Reisinger is but one of many associated resources at Harvard (not to mention the greater Boston area) for the study of the arts of Central and Northern Europe in all their fascinating diversity.

We have taken a somewhat unusual approach to our task, instead of offering a capsule history of the institution followed by a description of a certain number of the museum's more important works. The history of the museum is here told largely through the words of original documents. These documents, we hope, will give the reader a feeling for the time in which they were created and insight into the changing concerns of the museum and its curators over the years.

Similarly, the collections are described primarily from the point of view of how and when objects of certain kinds came to the Busch-Reisinger, rather than through an analysis of their art-historical significance. The selection of illustrations is also designed to give a sense of what may be found, enjoyed, and studied at the Busch-Reisinger. The full list of exhibitions mounted by and at the museum is not just a documentary record. It also affords a neutral overview of one important aspect of the museum's institutional memory, which does — and should — play an important role in influencing the nature of our current activities.

The closing annotated bibliography lists for the interested reader more conventional introductions to the museum, catalogues of its collections, essays on restricted aspects of its holdings, picture-book compendia, and similar guides.

It is probably true that, if the Busch-Reisinger did not already exist, there would be no compelling need to invent it. It would be unusual today to found a university art museum with the Busch-Reisinger's explicit limitation to one particular cultural region of Europe. Yet it has been Harvard's continuing task to find the productive potential in this wonderful "anomaly." This book not only shows how that has been achieved in the past; it also affirms the commitment to keep searching for creative ways in which the works of art in the museum's care can play a profound role in the lives of students, scholars, and the interested public.

SUMMARY CHRONOLOGY

(This provides a concise overview of institutional aspects of the museum. The history of acquisitions and exhibitions is laid out elsewhere in this publication.)

1897   A committee of three Harvard professors of German literature — among them Professor Kuno Francke — publishes an article, "The Need of a Germanic Museum at Harvard" (see p. 18).

1901   In the United States an "Association for the Establishment of a Germanic Museum in Cambridge, Massachusetts" is founded.

1902   While visiting Cambridge, where he receives an honorary degree, Prince Henry of Prussia announces that his brother Kaiser Wilhelm II "will make a magnificent gift to the Germanic Museum, which will include key monuments in the development of German sculpture."

1903   On the tenth of November — the birth date of Martin Luther and Friedrich Schiller — the dedication of the Germanic Museum in Rogers Hall takes place. Kuno Francke is curator (see p. 26).

1906   In honor of the Kaiser's silver wedding anniversary, Harvard announces an "Emperor William Fund." This gift of $30,000, donated by American friends of the Germanic Museum, is to be a financial basis for the institution. Adolphus Busch, a German-American brewer from St. Louis, becomes president of the Germanic Museum Association.

1910   After Adolphus Busch donates $265,000 for the construction of a new building, a design is commissioned from German Bestelmeyer of Dresden,

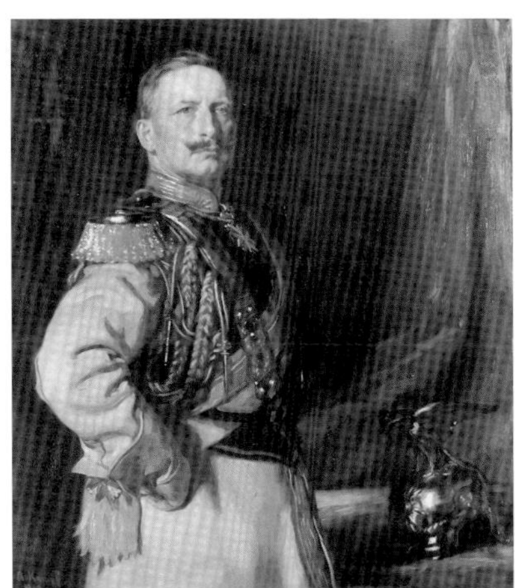

Arthur Kampf (1864–1950), **Portrait of Emperor Wilhelm II,** *1908.* **Oil, 102 x 89 cm. Gift of Mr. Hugo Reisinger, BR09.1.**

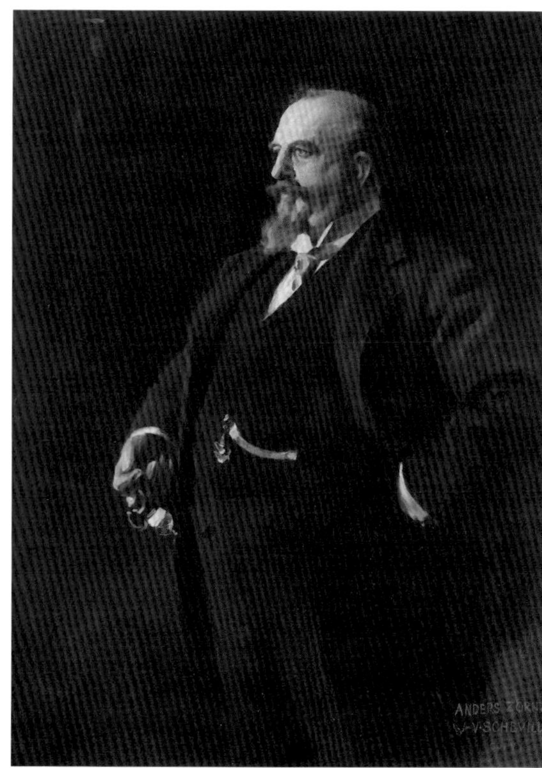

**W.V. Schevill (1864–1951),
Portrait of Adolphus
Busch,** *copy of the 1896
original by Anders Zorn.
Oil, 129.5 x 92.1 cm. Gift of
Mrs. Adolphus Busch,
BR25.2.*

a prominent historicist architect whose projects include the Central Hall of the University of Munich and an extension to the Germanisches Nationalmuseum in Nuremberg (see p. 35).

1912 After the ceremonial laying of a cornerstone in July, construction of the new building is delayed for two years because of legal problems with clearing the building site.

1913 Adolphus Busch dies.

1914 In July, a few weeks before the outbreak of World War I, construction is begun on the new Germanic Museum. Hugo Reisinger, the son-in-law of Adolphus Busch, dies; he bequeaths the museum an endowment of $50,000.

1916 Work on the new building takes place, with interruptions, in an atmosphere of increasingly anti-German feeling in the United States. Bestelmeyer never saw the building; construction was supervised by Langford Warren.

1917 The white plaster casts are moved to Busch Hall. After the United States enters the war against Germany and anti-German feelings reach a peak on campus, Francke resigns his professorship at Harvard and moves to the country. He retains his position as honorary curator of the Germanic Museum, which, however, remains closed for an indefinite time because of a "lack of coal."

1921   In April, Adolphus Busch Hall is dedicated and the Germanic Museum reopens. There are fifty thousand visitors in the first twelve months.

1927   The William Hayes Fogg Art Museum opens its new building on Quincy Street.

1927-28   As there is no specialist in German art at Harvard, two guest professors from Germany lecture, using the collection of the Germanic Museum: in 1927, Adolph Goldschmidt from the University of Berlin, and the following year, Gustav Pauli from the Kunsthalle in Hamburg.

1929   Before the crash of the stock market an endowment of $150,000 is raised for a Kuno Francke Professorship of German Art and Culture, a chair which continues today in Harvard's Department of Germanic Languages and Literatures.

1930   Kuno Francke dies on June 25. The Germanic Museum, which had been connected with the Department of Germanic Languages and Literatures since its founding, is placed under the supervision of the Fogg Art Museum and the Fine Arts Department, though the museums' visiting committees are not joined until 1964. Until then, the Busch-Reisinger is served by the visiting committee of the German Department. A young Harvard-trained art historian, Charles L. Kuhn, becomes curator with a part-time teaching appointment (see p. 29), and institutes the new policy of collecting original works of art from Central and Northern Europe. He also initiates a program of temporary exhibitions (see p. 21).

1935-37   Two murals are painted by Lewis W. Rubenstein, Harvard '30, in the foyer of Adolphus Busch Hall. The frescoes depict modern interpretations of ancient Nordic legends.

1937   An organ is installed in Adolphus Busch Hall's Romanesque Hall, a long-term loan from the Aeolian Skinner Company, at the behest of the celebrated organist E. Power Biggs. Biggs proceeds to play the complete organ works of J.S. Bach in twelve recitals at the museum.

1939   The Harvard Department of Germanic Languages and Literatures moves its offices into Adolphus Busch Hall. Kuhn is made associate professor of fine arts, becoming a full professor in 1955.

1939 The Curt von Faber du Faur Library of seven thousand German books (fifteenth to nineteenth centuries) is lent to the museum and installed in one of the galleries. The collection was eventually donated to Yale University.

1942 After the United States enters World War II, the Germanic Museum is closed again for an indefinite time. Its art collection and library are moved into storage at the Fogg. The building is used as a staff headquarters for the U.S. Army Chaplain School. E. Power Biggs gives weekly Sunday morning organ recitals which are broadcast nationwide by CBS Radio until 1958.

1946 At the end of the war, the museum is in a precarious financial position. Kuhn writes, "Most of the original works of art which have been deposited at the Fogg Museum during the past four years must remain in that institution for adequate care. The public lectures, concerts and elaborate loan exhibitions, which were regular features of the museum prior to the War, must to a large measure be discontinued." Kuhn proposes that the institution become a "study center for Germanic culture."

1947 Prompted by Fogg director John Coolidge, Kuhn begins to assemble a collection documenting the Bauhaus (see p. 77) with the assistance of Bauhaus founder Walter Gropius, who joined the faculty of Harvard's School of Architecture in 1937.

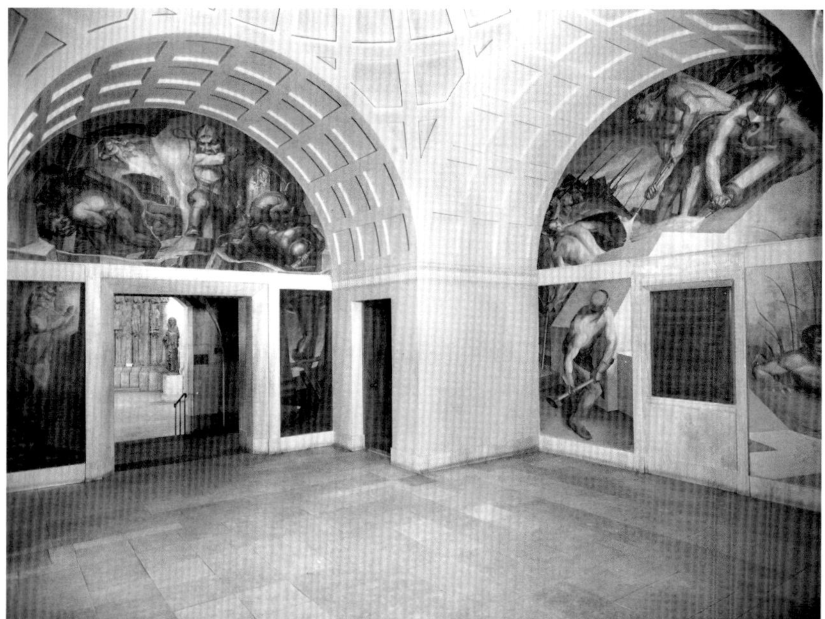

Murals, 1935–37, by Lewis Rubenstein, Harvard '30, in lobby of Adolphus Busch Hall

1948   A $5,000 donation from Edmée Busch Greenough, the daughter of Adolphus Busch, allows the museum again to augment and exhibit its holdings.

1949   A $200,000 donation is received from Edmée Busch Greenough. Kuhn becomes chairman of Harvard's Department of Fine Arts, a position he holds until 1953.

1950   In recognition of the enormous support from the Busch and Reisinger families through the years, the museum is renamed the Busch-Reisinger Museum of Germanic Culture (see p. 23). The largest exhibition hall is named "Kuno Francke Memorial Gallery."

1951   Plaster casts are removed from the small entrance gallery and are replaced with Gothic sculpture from the collection of the Fogg Art Museum.

1953   The Eda K. Loeb Endowment is established to support the curatorial activities of the museum.

1957   The German art historian Hans Maria Wingler does research on the museum's Bauhaus collection. The following year, as newly appointed director of the Bauhaus-Archiv in Darmstadt, Germany, and funded by the Rockefeller Foundation, Wingler returns as a research fellow.

   Kuhn defines his priorities in his annual report: "It is believed that the long term usefulness of the museum to the University programs of teaching and research will eventually depend on the extent and quality of the works of Germanic art available to teachers and scholars. The curator recognizes the importance of temporary exhibitions as an answer to the immediate needs of the University and as a stimulus to interest in the museum itself. Unfortunately the shortage of staff and of resources prevents the museum from pushing both aspects of its program with equal vigor. It becomes necessary, therefore, for acquisitions to take priority over the current program of activities."

1958   An organ by D.A. Flentrop of Zaandam, Holland, is first anonymously loaned, then donated to the museum. This instrument, designed to produce the pure and clear tone of the baroque organs on which Bach composed, is used by E. Power Biggs for concerts and recordings.

1958-59   The permanent collection in Adolphus Busch Hall is reinstalled, and only the most significant plaster casts remain on view. Original medieval art is installed in the "chapel" area, together with stained glass panels in the windows, lent by the Benedictine Priory of Portsmouth, R.I. Decorative arts occupy the ground level of the Francke Memorial Gallery, whose balcony accommodates twentieth-century art.

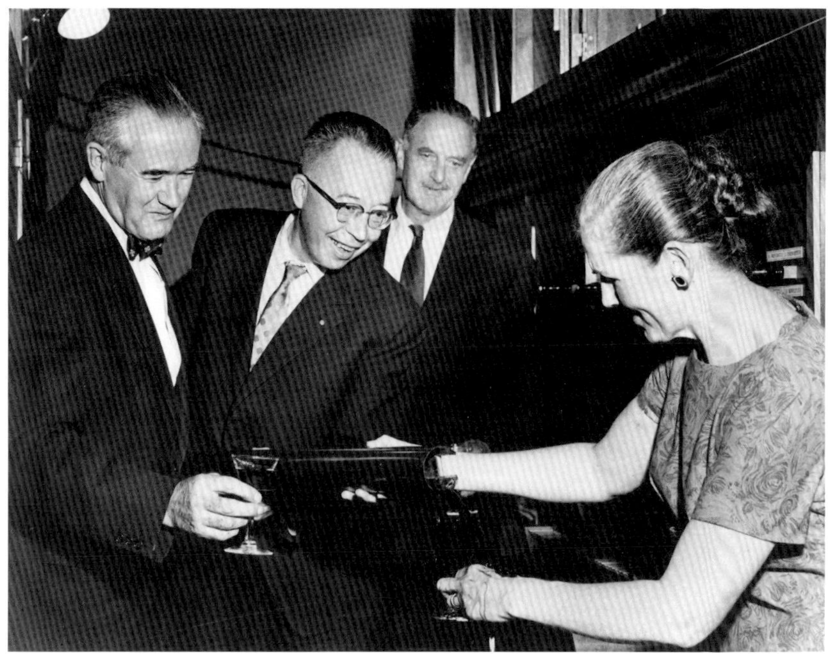

Dedication of Flentrop organ, 1958. Left to right: *E. Power Biggs, D.A. Flentrop, Charles Kuhn, and Mrs. Biggs. Champagne is being poured through an organ pipe.*

1960   Julia Phelps, lecturer in German, is acting curator for a year.

1961   Walter R. Davis establishes the Antonia Paepcke DuBrul Fund for the Acquisition of Works of Art.

1962   In this year (and again in 1963 and 1965), Kuhn selectively deaccessions certain paintings and works on paper from the modern collections.

1962-63   The Harvard Fine Arts Library is formed by merging the former Fogg and Busch-Reisinger Museum libraries with the fine arts collections from Harvard's Widener Library.

1963   The Feininger Archive is established (see p. 84). This resource includes 5,400 sketches, thousands of letters, unfinished canvases, photographs, and woodcuts given by the artist's widow. Further gifts of material for the Archive are received in 1965, 1971, and 1986.

1965   In an effort to consolidate and define the collections of both the Fogg and Busch-Reisinger Museums, early Flemish, Dutch, and German paintings and sculpture are transferred to the Busch-Reisinger Museum, and Central and Northern European prints are transferred to the Fogg. A "Care of Collections Endowment" for the museum is given by an anonymous donor.

1968   After thirty-eight years as curator, Charles Kuhn retires. In his concluding annual report, he writes that as "'Germanic' art is now regarded as one facet of a European cultural manifestation … the Busch-Reisinger's program should reflect this emphasis. … Future exhibitions illustrating the position of German art in Western Civilization would prove of enormous value to the study of cultural history." In honor of his retirement, the Charles L. Kuhn Endowment Fund is established, "to be devoted primarily to the presentation of significant exhibitions" at the museum.

1969   John David Farmer, a Renaissance scholar, becomes curator and lecturer in fine arts. Walter Gropius donates his archive to the museum. These materials include correspondence, drawings, prints, and photos documenting the first forty years of his architectural career (see p. 83).

1972   Hedy Landman, an art historian with a wide range of interests, becomes acting curator until 1974.

1974   Linda Seidel, a specialist in Romanesque sculpture, becomes acting curator and lecturer in fine arts. A proposal to make Adolphus Busch Hall into a museum for modern art encounters stiff opposition.

1975   Charles Werner Haxthausen, a specialist on Paul Klee, becomes curator and half-time professor until 1983. The Busch-Reisinger begins a fundraising campaign and serious discussions of the museum's future role. The Busch-Reisinger Museum Endowment Fund is established, "to bring the scholarly educational and exhibition program of the museum to the level merited by its growing collections …"

1978   Romanesque Hall is renamed in honor of Charles Kuhn. Gabriella Jeppson, an arts administrator specializing in modern art, is acting curator. During this year, and every year until the museum moves from Adolphus Busch Hall in 1987, the attendance averages thirty thousand.

1980-81   In an effort to increase the museum's visibility in the United States, masterpieces from the twentieth-century collection are shown at the National Gallery in Washington and the Wildenstein Gallery in New York (total attendance 130,000).

1981   The Volkswagen Foundation establishes a five-year visiting professorship program for prominent scholars from Germany to do research at the museum and teach in Harvard's Fine Arts Department.

1982-83   In a campaign to make the museum better known across the Atlantic, masterpieces from the twentieth-century collection are shown in Germany at the Städel in Frankfurt, the Bauhaus-Archiv in Berlin, and

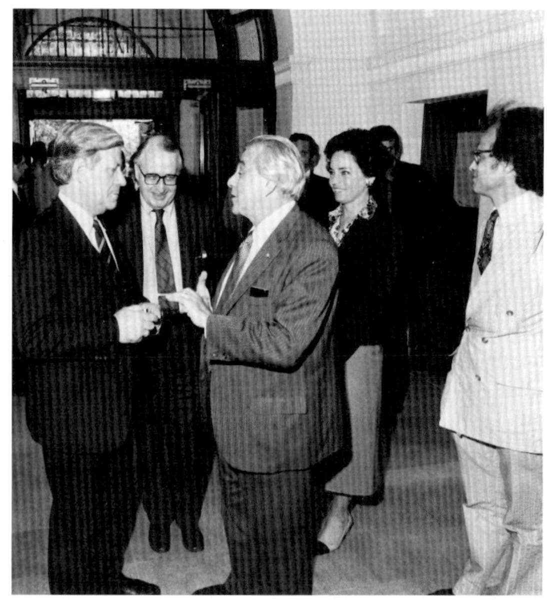

Helmut Schmidt (left), Chancellor of Germany, visiting the museum at the time of his honorary degree from Harvard in 1979. To the right of Chancellor Schmidt are Dean Henry Rosovsky, Prof. Seymour Slive, Gabriella Jeppson, and Prof. Konrad Oberhuber.

the Kunstmuseum Düsseldorf. The exhibition is seen by 70,500 viewers in these three cities.

1983 Peter Nisbet becomes curator. A Friends of the Busch-Reisinger Museum foundation is established in the Federal Republic of Germany. By 1991 this association numbers some two hundred members in Germany, Austria, and Switzerland.

1985 The Arthur M. Sackler Museum opens to house the Art Museums' collections of Islamic, Asian, and ancient art.

1986 A decision is made to work towards a new building for the Busch-Reisinger Museum, attached to the Fogg Art Museum. The Daimler-Benz company, in honor of its centennial, donates funds to endow the curatorship of the Busch-Reisinger Museum.

1987 The Busch-Reisinger Museum moves into temporary quarters in the Fogg while awaiting completion of the new building. The back galleries, basement, and upper floors of Adolphus Busch Hall are renovated and leased to Harvard's Minda de Gunzburg Center for European Studies. The Harvard University Art Museums retain control of the medieval galleries, which include the Flentrop organ. The Busch-Reisinger Museum donates nineteenth-century Swedish peasant furniture and objects (acquired in 1952) to the American Swedish Institute in Minneapolis. The government of the Federal Republic of Germany initiates a five-year program to support the expenses for the museum's curatorial staff.

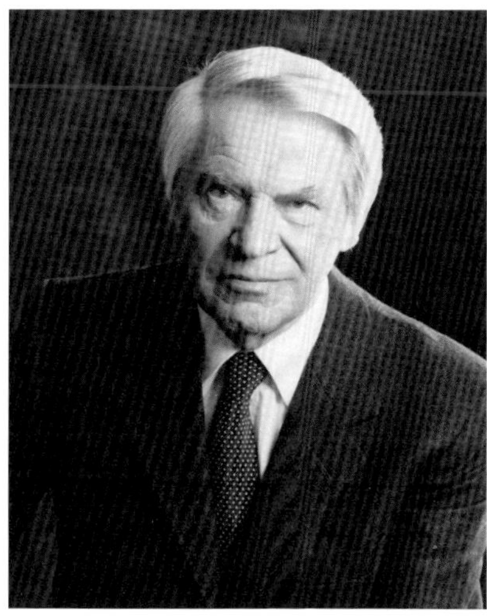

Dr. Werner Otto, principal donor of Werner Otto Hall.

1988   Gwathmey Siegel & Associates of New York is chosen to design the new building for the Busch-Reisinger Museum, to be named Werner Otto Hall in honor of its principal donor. The Otto Hall project also encompasses the Susan Morse Hilles Reading Room for the Fine Arts Library, new office space for library staff on two levels, and the Philip and Lynn Straus Gallery for works of art on paper in the Fogg building. Peter Nisbet is appointed the museum's first Daimler-Benz Curator.

1991   Werner Otto Hall is dedicated on September 28–29 and opens to the public on October 1.

STATEMENTS OF PURPOSE

The Need of a Germanic Museum at Harvard (1897)

This programmatic statement was written in March 1897 by a special committee of Harvard's German Department, consisting of George Bartlett, Kuno Francke, and Hugo K. Schilling. Published as a pamphlet, the statement lays out the conception which was to become a reality with the founding of the Germanic Museum in 1901 and the subsequent enthusiastic support of the idea by Kaiser Wilhelm II.

Not so very long ago the study of German in this country was valued chiefly as a means of acquiring facility in reading or speaking a language which has come to be of great practical importance in professional, business, and scholarly pursuits. Indeed, in some parts of the country this is still the prevailing view taken not only of the study of German, but of all modern languages. Greek and Latin are still surrounded with the halo of a time when all higher culture was considered to be bound up with a knowledge of Greek and Roman life; while French and German are not infrequently looked upon as upstarts whose standing in the hierarchy of learning is not yet beyond doubt.

It is, however, clear that for some generations past a change has been gradually coming. The first impulse, as far as German is concerned, was given by the great epoch of German literature at the beginning of this century. When Bancroft and Hedge and Motley returned from their studies at German universities, they brought with them not only a fuller equipment of scholarship, but also a strong enthusiasm for the noble intellectual movement which was then shaping the destiny of modern Germany. Following this, there came the influence of 1848; the March–revolution struck a chord to which the American heart vibrated; and when the martyrs of this revolution sought a refuge in this country, they found here a ready welcome and intelligent sympathy with German aspirations. In the friendship between Longfellow and Freiligrath this twofold affinity between the two countries as to both literary and political ideals may be said to have received its most notable symbolic expression. Next there followed the general adoption of German methods of scientific research brought here by the steadily growing number of American teachers, physicians, theologians who had received the decisive stimulus for their life's work at the universities of Berlin, Göttingen, or Heidelberg. And finally, the dominant position acquired by Germany since the war of 1870 gave the American people a new sense of the dignity of the German nation, and kindled interest in the history of the Teutonic race.

There exists, then, to-day an ever-increasing disposition on the part of Americans to approach the study of German as a study leading to an insight into a great national civilization. Of the rapidity with which this tendency is developing, the history of the German Department of Harvard University during the last twenty-five years is an index. In 1871–72 there were given two elective courses in German, both of a miscellaneous character. The number of students enrolled in them was 100. Of departmental organization, hardly a beginning had been made. … The number of courses offered, apart from the prescribed course in Elementary German, is twenty-nine. … The number of students enrolled in these elective courses is about 750.

Gratifying as this development is, it brings into clear relief the need of further important improvements. To one of these, namely: the need of a Germanic Museum, we wish to call the attention of the community at large.

It is a principle now generally accepted that a nation's history cannot be studied adequately without a consideration of its achievements in the monumental and domestic arts. Nowhere does the spirit of a people manifest itself more clearly and impressively than in the buildings devoted to public worship or public deliberations, in the images embodying the popular conception of sacred legend or national tradition, in the appliances for private comfort and security. To the student of Greek and Roman culture nearly all the higher institutions of learning offer at least some possibility of making himself acquainted with the principal monuments of Greek and Roman art. The student of Semitic civilization has an excellent opportunity of examining Assyrian and Babylonian monuments in our own Semitic Museum. The Boston Museum of Fine Arts, in its Japanese collection, gives an admirable conspectus of national life in the Far East. Both the Boston Museum of Fine Arts and the Fogg Art Museum at Harvard contain valuable collections illustrating certain phases of mediaeval and Renaissance art. But nowhere in this country is there a chance of studying consecutively even the most important monuments of Germanic civilization. Nowhere in this country can the student obtain a vivid impression of the life and customs of our forefathers, from early Teutonic times to the later Middle Ages, such as is afforded by the "Germanisches Museum" at Nuremberg and other European collections. Nowhere can be given an accurate conception of the wonderful Romanesque cathedrals of the twelfth century, of the extraordinary power of German sculpture in the thirteenth, of the exquisite works of German wood-carving in the fourteenth and fifteenth centuries — or even of the work of such great men as Peter Vischer and Albrecht Dürer.

In suggesting the establishment at Harvard of a Museum devoted to this hitherto neglected subject, we do not wish to enter into a discussion of the aesthetic value of German art. We admit that for the cultivation of the sense of formal beauty the study of Italian art is decidedly more important than the study of German art; although we should not be willing to grant this preference to the art of any other modern nation. What we maintain is the paramount importance of such a collection as this for the study of civilization.

Four or five rooms containing views and reproductions of characteristic works of Germanic industry and art from the earliest times to the sixteenth century might form a satisfactory beginning of such a museum. First in the collection, chronologically, would be photographs and casts of such objects from the neolithic age as may serve to throw light upon the questions of the existence of an anthropologically distinct Teutonic race, of its previous history and of its geographical distribution in Europe. Next there would follow specimens of the characteristic products of the Hallstatt and La Tène periods; models of the earliest habitations in Germanic territory, so far as their construction can be ascertained from actual remains, from imitations in the form of house-urns, and from the descriptions of ancient writers; pictures showing the mode of burial in various epochs, and casts of tombstones with Runic inscriptions. The progress made during the period of the Migrations and the centuries immediately following, in the arts of working metals, of carving and weaving, would be shown by reproductions of objects in the museums of Nuremberg, Mainz, and Christiania, and in the British Museum; the development of navigation by models of boats, from the dug-out of the lake-dweller to the sea-going boat of Nydam and the Viking ship of Gokstad; the advance in architecture by models of the German, the Anglo-Saxon, and the Norse halls as described in the literatures of the respective countries. German culture during the period from Charlemagne to the Hohenstaufen would be illustrated by photographs of exteriors and interiors of the great Romanesque cathedrals of Aachen, Worms, Speier, Mainz, etc., the Kaiserpfalz at Goslar, the Wartburg and other castles, and by casts of such works of sculpture as the Bernward column of Hildesheim, the brass portals of Hildesheim and Augsburg, the Lion of Braunschweig, etc., etc. The thirteenth century would be characterized by photographs of the great Gothic cathedrals, and by photographs or casts of the sculptures at Freiberg, Wechselburg, Naumburg, Bamberg, Freiburg, Strassburg. For the fourteenth century a selection of sepulchral monuments from the "Germanisches Museum" at Nuremberg would be sufficient; while the fifteenth century should be fully brought to view by representative types of the earlier wood-carving, by specimens of the various schools of painting between the Van Eycks and Dürer, and, finally, by as complete a collection as possible of the works of Dürer, Holbein, Peter Vischer, Adam Krafft, Veit Stoss, Michael Pacher and Hans Brüggemann.

A collection like this could hardly be begun with less than $10,000. But, if carried out successfully, it would undoubtedly be one of the most useful departments of the University. It would be the first attempt to bring before the eyes of American students a picture of early European and mediaeval civilization. It would, at the same time, be a worthy monument to the genius of a people which has had a large part in shaping the ideals of modern life and which has given to this country millions of devoted citizens.

The New Policy of the Germanic Museum (1932)

Published in the Harvard Alumni Bulletin, *February 19, 1932, this statement by the new curator Charles Kuhn spelled out the decisive changes in policy which have determined the course of the museum ever since.*

The Germanic Museum has been able to develop in many directions because of its alliance with the other art museums of the University. This was brought about by a reorganization modeled on the system long in use by the University libraries, all the various special libraries being under one general directorship. Similarly, the directors of the Fogg Museum have been made directors of the Semitic and Germanic Museums, with curators appointed to act as field generals. The step was taken to prevent duplication of effort, to encourage cooperation, and to centralize the educational endeavors in art and archaeology. The result has been that the Germanic Museum has become an active institution, playing a definite part in the artistic life of the community.

The collections of books and photographs are rapidly being developed. Several thousand photographs of German, Flemish, and Scandinavian art have been acquired and carefully catalogued. Duplicate cards are filed at the Fogg Museum so that the records of all the photographic material of the University dealing with the fine arts are to be found in one place. The acquisition of this material will permit the Fogg Museum to concentrate its efforts along other than Germanic lines. Books have been purchased with a similar purpose in view. A small but interesting collection of books and photographs dealing with contemporary German art has been formed.

Professor Kuno Francke, the founder and first curator of the Germanic Museum, saw the labors of his lifetime bear fruit in the establishment of the professorship that carries his name. The purpose of this professorship is to bring some great Germanic scholar to Harvard to help promote an understanding of German culture. Naturally this plays an important part in the affairs of the Museum. The first incumbent of the chair was Professor Adolph Goldschmidt of the University of Berlin. During the year 1930–1931 he conducted courses in various phases of German art. The students made considerable use of the material at the Germanic Museum for these courses …

Another very important activity of the Germanic Museum is the holding of loan exhibitions. These give the students an opportunity to see and study original works of art gathered from widely separated localities and brought together to illustrate some specific school or tendency. The first exhibition, held in January, 1931, presented a review of German etching, engraving, and woodcutting from earliest times to the present day. A carefully selected group of over a hundred prints were on exhibition; they showed a logical development in German graphic art from the beginnings in the fifteenth century, through the great masters such as Dürer and Holbein, to the most recent products of contemporary artists.

In the spring there followed an exhibition of drawings by Dutch masters of the seventeenth century. Such eminent painters as Rembrandt, Ruysdael, and Ostade were generously represented.

The exhibition calendar for the current academic year is full and varied. At the present writing the Museum is holding an exhibition of the sculpture and drawings of George Kolbe, who is perhaps the greatest of living German sculptors. This is to be followed by exhibitions of modern Hungarian painting, the advertising work of the Luebeck artist, Alfred Mahlau, and paintings by the Little Dutch Masters of the seventeenth century.

It will be seen from the program outlined above that the term "Germanic" is interpreted in a very broad sense. The Museum attempts to promote an interest, not only in German art, but also in the artistic production of such related countries as Austria, Switzerland, Norway, Sweden, Denmark, Hungary, Holland, and Belgium. Even certain phases of English, Burgundian, and Norman art come under the category of Germanic.

A similarly broad interpretation is used in the acquisition of objects as part of the permanent collection of the Museum. The original purpose of the institution was to illustrate the development of Germanic art by means of reproductions. This policy is being followed and is proving of great value for teaching purposes. A collection of some 75 reproductions of German and Flemish paintings has been purchased to illustrate a few of the masterpieces of north European painting. The acquisition of a group of reproductions of Merovingian jewelry gives the student an opportunity to study the production of Germanic lands in the early Middle Ages.

In spite of the teaching value of these reproductions, the fundamental aesthetic appeal is lacking. The student may be able to see stylistic tendencies and developments, but the spark of beauty, which is the fundamental reason for the study of art, cannot be reproduced. In order to stimulate a real appreciation of Germanic art, one must deal with originals. Therefore, an important part of the new policy of the Germanic Museum is to acquire a small but representative collection of original works of art.

Through the generosity of friends of the Museum, a modest start already has been made in this direction. A new room of contemporary German and Scandinavian decorative art has been opened. It contains pottery, glass, metal work, advertising posters, and textiles which illustrate the great beauty in modern commercial design. An important work of sculpture by Ernst Barlach has been installed in the courtyard, and a self-portrait by Renée Sintenis graces the entrance of the decorative art room.

It is far too early to judge the value of the new policy of the Germanic Museum, but certain indications seem to point to its soundness. There has been an increased interest in Germanic art among the undergraduates. Several graduate students have been inspired to do research work in the field of Germanic art. Lastly, the number of visitors to the Museum has greatly increased. During the first three months of the current year the attendance has numbered approximately 5,800.

Through the collection of books and photographs, through exhibitions, concerts, public lectures, the acquisition of original works of art, the publishing of scholarly literature, and the establishment of a system of scholarships, the Germanic Museum hopes some day to become the great center in America for the study of north European culture.

Announcement by Charles L. Kuhn, on the change of the museum's name (1950)

Released to the press on May 8, 1950, this announcement not only gives reasons for the change in the museum's name, but also spells out Kuhn's conception of the museum's function at a time when it was finally finding a secure and active role for itself. It is worth noting that the name of the museum was changed again in 1981 to the Busch-Reisinger Museum of Central and Northern European Art, ratifying an informal usage already prevalent for several years. In 1990, the President and Fellows of Harvard College simplified the name to the Busch-Reisinger Museum.

This is to inform you that on February 6, 1950, the President and Fellows of Harvard University voted to change the name of the Germanic Museum to the Busch-Reisinger Museum of Germanic Culture in recognition of the long continued interest of members of the Busch and Reisinger families in the study of Germanic Culture at Harvard.

The change of name will in no way affect the policy of the institution. The Museum will continue, by means of temporary exhibitions, to bring before the student body and the general public significant trends in the visual arts of all countries. The collections of original works of art and of research material will be devoted, as in the past, to illustrating the cultural development of Germany, Scandinavia, Austria, Switzerland and the Low Countries.

The headquarters of the Department of Germanic Languages and Literatures will continue to be located in the Museum Building.

The Role of the Harvard Art Museums (1990)

This "mission statement" was prepared by Harvard President Derek Bok in November 1990, after extensive consultation with museum staff, faculty, and other interested parties. It was written as part of a longer document describing the duties and qualifications of the director of the Harvard University Art Museums. As one of those museums, the Busch-Reisinger Museum's task of promoting the informed enjoyment and critical understanding of the arts of Central and Northern Europe is undertaken within these broader terms of the overall mission.

The basic mission of the Harvard University Art Museums, as for all museums, is to acquire, preserve, interpret, exhibit, and otherwise make accessible works of art for the benefit of a variety of interested audiences, recognizing that art is fully understood and enjoyed through direct contact with original works of genuine aesthetic merit. Those who direct university museums can usually identify a number of audiences which they try to serve. These audiences include professors and students of Fine Arts, faculty and students in other departments of the University, visiting scholars, and the general public.

A university art museum such as Harvard's serves all of these audiences. To a large extent, the needs of each can be addressed by carrying out the fundamental educational mission of the museum, and an imaginative director will seek to do so insofar as possible. Priorities need to be established, particularly when financial resources are limited. The Harvard University Art Museums exist principally for educational reasons and thus owe their primary responsibility to students and faculty at Harvard.

The concern for education should characterize and inform every aspect of the Harvard University Art Museums. For example:

1. The Harvard art museums should measure their success primarily by the extent to which they are drawn upon by faculty and students from all parts of the University to enrich classes, seminars, research, and other means of understanding art. Their principal measure of achievement is the amount of learning that is brought about or enhanced by their collections. Although good didactic exhibitions will also attract the general public and garner favorable reviews by critics, public attendance and critical praise should be considered integral outcomes of an educational job well done rather than primary objectives in and of themselves.

2. It is understood that different kinds of exhibitions may be valuable in illuminating various approaches to understanding art or culture, some of which may require choosing objects for other than aesthetic reasons. In such cases, the educational purposes of the museums should be overriding.

Whatever the exhibition, high aesthetic standards in the display of objects should be maintained, since they attract the viewer's interest and enhance learning and enjoyment. A well-presented show, regardless of the nature of the objects themselves, also provides a model for museum professionals and students interested in museum careers. Nevertheless, in particular areas of the museum and at particular times, the educational mission may come into conflict with the appearance of the museums. For example, designated galleries may have to be hung and rehung repeatedly to serve the purposes of a particular course. In such cases, the museums should accommodate the needs of the course as effectively as possible.

3. Harvard museums should try to involve students in all phases of museum activity — in conservation labs, in planning exhibitions, in undertaking research for collections and catalogues. Ideally, the only restraint upon student involvement should be consideration of conservation of the work of art; indeed, this absolute priority is an integral part of education in this field.

Where appropriate, faculty should be encouraged to include objects from the museums in their courses and to engage students in study of original works of art. The more students are seriously involved in these ways, the better the museums are fulfilling their mission.

4. It is a special responsibility of the Harvard museums to prepare talented young people to become museum professionals. No institution is in a better position to assume this function than a university museum, and no university museum is better equipped for the task than Harvard's Art Museums. The Fine Arts Department should encourage graduate students (and applicants for admission) who may be interested in museum careers just as strongly as those who are pursuing faculty careers. The academic training for both museum and faculty careers should be equally rigorous with the same intellectual standards.

5. As part of the larger University community, the art museums should also reach out to students who are not enrolled in Fine Arts courses, particularly

undergraduates. The museums can play an important educational role for these students, particularly those who may not have had much prior exposure to great works of art in the original.

6. To fulfill their educational purposes, Harvard museums need not (and cannot) show all or even the largest part of their collections. It is their responsibility, however, to continue to make sure that all objects are readily accessible for study by students and scholars. Since large public museums can rarely match this degree of accessibility to works of art in storage, a university museum has a special obligation to the scholarly world to provide this kind of service.

7. Due to limits of space, Harvard museums should continue to adhere to a thoughtful acquisition policy that limits new accessions to works of substantial educational value. The director and curators are responsible for ensuring that all works that enter the museums' collections are germane to the University's mission of teaching and research and have been acquired in accordance with stated University and professional standards of ethics.

Priority in the museums' collections is given to:

— works of high artistic quality that can be displayed in public galleries and that help illuminate a significant art historical period or personality;

— works which, because of their materials, technique, or condition or because of their historical, archaeological, or anthropological pertinence to significant art historical periods may be of special value to academic study or to the understanding of works of high artistic quality already in the collections, insofar as they would not be included within the accessions of other Harvard museums and collections.

8. The curators of a university teaching museum should fully support the museum's educational mission through research, publication, teaching, working with students, and collaborative relationships with faculty. Research leading to innovative exhibitions, catalogues, and scholarly papers can serve as a resource to develop or enhance academic courses as well as make a contribution to art historical scholarship.

9. Like all academic institutions, the art museums should participate actively in scholarly dialogues nationally and internationally. Through independent efforts as well as collaborative work with faculty members and other colleagues, the curatorial staff should engage in ongoing art historical discourse through publications, traveling exhibitions, lectures, academic reviews, and other forms of communication.

KUNO FRANCKE & CHARLES KUHN

Clearly, the two decisive personalities in establishing the character of the Busch-Reisinger Museum were Professor Kuno Francke, curator of the museum from 1903 to 1929, and Professor Charles L. Kuhn, curator from 1930 to 1968. The following two texts are the "Minutes on the Life and Services" of the two men, prepared by the Faculty of Arts and Sciences.

In addition to the decades-long tenures of Francke and Kuhn, other curators (acting, assistant, associate, or full) have been: Julia Phelps (1960–61), John David Farmer (1969–71), Hedy Landman (1972–74), Linda Seidel (1974–75), Charles Werner (Mark) Haxthausen (1975–83), Gabriella Jeppson (1978–79), and Peter Nisbet (since 1983).

Not insignificant roles in the history of the Busch-Reisinger have been played by the directors of the Fogg — or, since 1985, of the Harvard University Art Museums. Sometimes with administrative authority over the Busch-Reisinger, these have included Paul Sachs, Edward Forbes, Arthur Pope, John Coolidge, Agnes Mongan, Daniel Robbins, Seymour Slive, John Rosenfield, Edgar Peters Bowron, Marjorie Cohn, and James Cuno.

Kuno Francke

The Harvard "obituary" for Kuno Francke was written by Frank William Taussig, William Guild Howard, and Taylor Stark. It was placed in the official record on January 20, 1931, and published in the Harvard University Gazette *on January 24, 1931.*

Kuno Francke, Professor of the History of German Culture, was born at Kiel, Schleswig-Holstein, on September 27, 1855, and died in Cambridge, June 25, 1930. The stock was of the German intellectual class; the grandfather was a university professor, the father was on the bench. The son grew up in an environment of thrift, unremitting industry, obedience to duty and conscience, respect for the higher life. His education was of the sort traditional in Germany — the exacting gymnasium, lectures and seminaries at several universities, independent delving of his own into sources. After taking the degree of Ph.D. at Munich in 1878, he became one of the notable group who under Waitz edited the Monumenta Germaniae Historica. The subject of his doctoral dissertation was in the field of medieval poetry and folklore. Such specialization during his formative

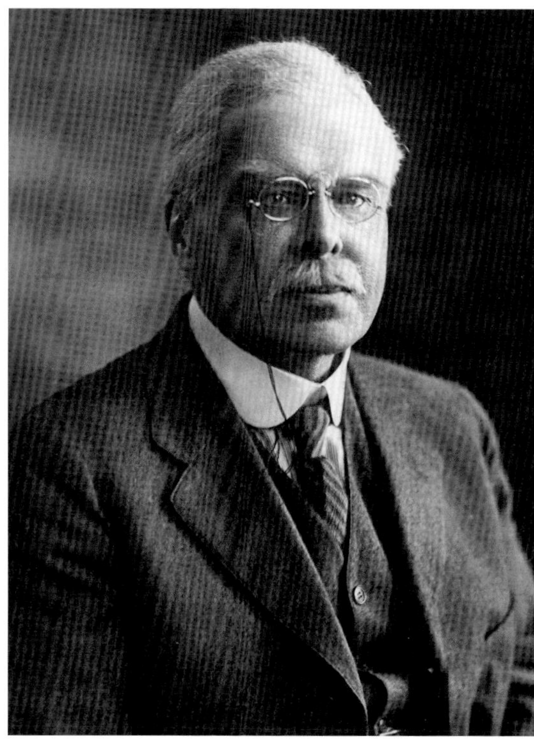

Kuno Francke

years laid the foundation for a wide command of history, and was the first stage in the acquisition of a scholarly equipment remarkable for extent and thoroughness. It ranged through the centuries, and for every period showed scrupulous accuracy as well as powers of broad generalization.

While still a student at Berlin in 1875, Francke fell in with Ephraim Emerton, and a friendship grew up which lasted through life. Professor Emerton was impressed by the younger scholar's breadth of interest and aptitude in letters, and brought him to the attention of President Eliot. He came to Harvard University in 1884 as instructor in German, became assistant professor in 1887, professor in 1896. It was fortunate that he transplanted himself. While he never failed in love for his fatherland or in appreciation and defence of its high traditions, he was always at heart democratic, opposed to caste and privilege; and the social and academic atmosphere of pre-war Germany was charged with much that was alien to him. In his adopted country he found a life more free and at the same time educational and scholarly opportunities that allowed scope for his special gifts.

Year after year, from 1884 to 1916, Francke gave at this university courses which covered the history of German Literature, Art, and Thought. They traversed the Middle Ages, the Mysticism of the 14th Century, the Crusades, the Renaissance, the Reformation, the golden 18th century, down to the present era. Keen as he was to appreciate the significance of every period, his feelings were warmest for the work of Goethe. Everything in literature he related to the wider intellectual currents; to art, philosophy, political speculation. He taught history in the best sense.

As a lecturer and teacher Francke was more than effective and impressive. He had a kindling quality. Tho far from pretentious or theatrical — indeed by temperament modest — he yet had an oratorical bent. When he read or lectured, his voice rose, his eye brightened, there was spontaneous cadence and emphasis. He was welcome and admired as a public lecturer. His style was in accord with this trait; it had sweep and buoyancy. His sense of the structure and music of language showed itself in his English writings, but naturally most of all in his native German.

Scholar though he was, his nature was that of a poet. What a man loves is as significant as what he does; and the singularly beautiful bits of verse quoted in his history of German literature show the choice of one who was himself a craftsman. His verses, not many, and all of later date, were not publicly printed until gathered into a thin volume in 1923. They are lyrics, delicately fashioned, deeply expressive whether of hope or sorrow. His idealistic nature showed itself in his contact with students, colleagues, friends. Men of all kinds found a friendly welcome, and warm appreciation of their work and thought. Nothing was further from him than professional jealousy, and nothing gave him greater pleasure than the achievements of his associates. The catastrophe of the great war fell heavily on him. His understanding of what was good on both sides, and his open mind toward different points of view, brought him at the time more criticism than forbearance or sympathy. It was an inestimable solace in his closing years that the passions of the war had cooled, and bitterness of feeling ceased.

Francke's publications were many. Best known are the volume Social Forces in German Literature, later enlarged into A History of German Literature as determined by Social Forces; and the great treatise (in German) on Die Kulturwerte der deutschen Literatur, of which two volumes, bringing the account to the middle of the 18th century, were completed by 1923. The first instalment of the third volume, on Weltbürgertum in der deutschen Literatur, was published in 1928; a second instalment, which was to bear the title Nationalismus in der deutschen Literatur, lay half finished on his desk. A number of smaller books, the outgrowth of articles in periodicals and lectures, appeared between 1907 and 1930, some in German, some in English. The very last among them was an autobiographical sketch written in 1929 at the insistent request of a publisher.

Honors came to him plenteously. Harvard University made him in 1912 an Honorary Doctor of Letters. The University of Wisconsin made him a Doctor of Laws, and the University of Munich an Honorary Ph.D. He was honorary member and Senator in the Deutsche Akademie at Munich, and was similarly distinguished by the Deutsche Gesellschaft für Soziologie; and was Fellow of the American Academy of Arts and Sciences, the American Philosophical Society, the Medieval Academy of America. The Germanic Museum at this University is a monument to him; the conception and execution were his, and the gifts which made it possible flowed from admiration for the man as well as for what he represented. The museum is unique in that it gives the visitor, by means of perfect reproductions, a picture of the development of German sculpture, a goal which could never have been attained had its founder attempted to collect originals. Most enduring among his distinctions, and most dear to him, was the establishment in 1929 of the Kuno Francke Professorship of German Art and Culture; a foundation which happily commemorates for all time a career of strenuous service and high achievement, and a nature of wonderful sweetness.

Charles L. Kuhn

The "Memorial Minute" for Charles Kuhn was written by John Coolidge, Mark Haxthausen, Julia Phelps, John Rosenfield, Seymour Slive, and Neil Levine (chairman). It was adopted on May 19, 1987, and published in the Harvard University Gazette *on July 17, 1987.*

Charles Louis Kuhn was born in Cincinnati on December 14, 1901, and died in Cambridge on July 21, 1985. His family were financiers and reputedly quite conservative. Kuhn, somewhat fractious, was sent to a military school. A double reaction ensued: he rejected his family's conventional aesthetic values; he became the gentlest, the least military of men.

Kuhn received an A.B. from the University of Michigan in 1923. He then came to Harvard for graduate study in Fine Arts and was awarded his Ph.D. in 1929. His dissertation was published as *Romanesque Painting of Catalonia.*

During his graduate student years there were in Cambridge some remarkable young enthusiasts for contemporary art, men such as Alfred Barr, Russell Hitchcock, "Chick" Austin, Edward Warburg, Lincoln Kirstein, and Alexander Calder. Their contribution to this country's present concern with the art of our time is inestimable. Kuhn's particular role was introducing to Francophile America the achievements of the German avant-garde.

For Kuhn, 1930 was the climactic year. In March he married Hetty Shuman; in July he was appointed curator of what was then Harvard's Germanic Museum. This he remained until his retirement in 1968.

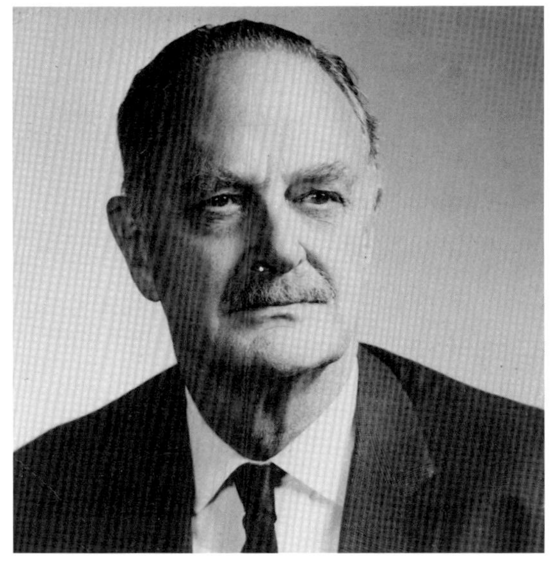

Charles L. Kuhn, ca. 1956

The first need, of course, was to raise funds, no easy task while the Great Depression was deepening and the Third Reich became increasingly threatening. But from the start, and throughout the next thirty-eight years, Kuhn always kept the museum's budget in balance. That success was achieved jointly with his wife. It required unflagging devotion of time and effort as well as occasional silent contributions of their own money. The long-term results were important funds for acquisitions and a capital grant so substantial that the museum was renamed in honor of the donors, the Busch-Reisinger family.

As for activities, an initial step was to organize temporary exhibitions. As early as 1932 he presented a broad survey of contemporary German painting. Then followed monographic shows of Albers, Kandinsky, Klee, and other artists. All were displayed with exceptional sensitivity. There were in addition lecture series, concerts, and films. Kuhn did ninety percent of the preparatory work himself, for his staff at the museum was rarely more than a single guard and a part-time secretary.

The public reaction was immediate and favorable. Already in October 1931, the *Boston Transcript* noted the museum "shaking the dust of antiquity from its collections to make way for art of contemporary interest."

What were those collections? The museum had been founded [i.e., opened] in 1903 by Professor Kuno Francke to be the handmaiden of the Department of Germanic Languages and Literature. The galleries, as Kuhn found them, were filled with plaster casts of German art. There were but two originals, a standard portrait of Kaiser Wilhelm II and a tapestry unworthy of exhibition. All the original works of art now in the Busch-Reisinger Museum were either acquired for it by Kuhn or obtained after his retirement in continuation of his policies.

There was nothing timid about Kuhn. He began by weeding the collection of casts, for, as he wrote of them at the time: "the student may be able to see stylistic tendencies and developments, but the spark of beauty cannot be reproduced." Those he retained represent such familiar classics as Duke Henry's Lion, the entire "golden" portal of Freiberg, and Peter Fischer's King Arthur. These he gradually supplemented with original works of art, whether by purchase, bequest, or long-term loan. In contrast to the replicas of classic monuments, the originals exemplify the art of expiring styles, be it the splendor or the agonized intensity of northern late Gothic, be it the courtly elegance or the up-country religious fervor of late German Baroque. An especial interest were the varied media of the decorative arts.

But Kuhn's greatest curatorial achievement was to assemble a collection of Expressionism, Germany's first contribution to the art of the twentieth century. Finding them "degenerate," Hitler had taken from the museums of his nation the finest examples of its contemporary art and put them on the market. Thus they became available to perceptive collectors like Kuhn. The group of drawings, sculpture, prints, and paintings he assembled is today considered outstanding in Germany itself. In addition, Walter Gropius arrived in Cambridge in 1938 and helped him assemble works by former Bauhaus colleagues.

Kuhn's dedication attracted notable gifts to the Busch-Reisinger. Remarkable among these were Gropius' own papers, the archives of Lyonel Feininger, a splendid group of Barlach's, and a magnificent Flentrop organ presented by the internationally known performer E. Power Biggs.

Simply put, the Busch-Reisinger Museum presents almost a thousand years of German art in a way that is unrivaled outside their country of origin.

Aspects of this achievement were made known by scholarly articles on special works in the museum collections and by two indispensable catalogues: *German Expressionism and Abstract Art, the Harvard Collections* (1957) and *German and Netherlandish Sculpture 1280–1800, the Harvard Collections* (1965).

Charles Kuhn began teaching in 1931 and continued to do so until he retired. His specialty was art of the northern Renaissance, witness his book *A Catalogue Raisonnée of German Paintings of the Middle Ages and the Renaissance in American Collections*. When acquiring works of art he always asked: "How effective will this object be in teaching?" To a remarkable degree he incorporated into his courses works of art his students could see in local collections.

As a lecturer he was lucid and informative. Invariably the starting points were the purpose and place of the work of art, as well as the period and career of the artist. Exceptionally shy and genuinely modest, he spoke without rhetoric or hyperbole, yet he subtly revealed his own responses to the masterpieces he was discussing.

Kuhn made graduate students aware of the need of a background as broad as his own. Having exemplified the appropriate ways to deal with special topics he left his seminar pupils largely independent in their research. The realization of the responsibility involved was for each a lifelong gain.

Kuhn served as Chairman of the Department of Fine Arts from 1949 to 1953. Also he was for a full four-year term the editor of the leading American scholarly journal in our field, the *Art Bulletin*. All in all, Charles Kuhn was the most versatile person who has ever taught the history of art at Harvard.

As a friend, two qualities in particular come to mind. He was a superb judge of character. He helped shape the careers of many men and women who later achieved distinction in the teaching and museum professions.

A quiet firmness was of his very nature. He invariably reached his objectives without confrontation. Always willing to hear about your problems, he would, when asked, explain how you could most effectively overcome them. In short, he was that rare combination, a perceptive, wise, and warmhearted man.

The Museum's Buildings

Rogers Hall

Built as Harvard's first gymnasium in 1859 to designs by E.C. Cabot, this octagonal building, 74 feet across, stood on the triangle of Cambridge Street, Broadway, and Quincy Street, about equidistant between the museum's second home, Adolphus Busch Hall, and its present home in Werner Otto Hall. With the completion in 1878 of other athletic facilities, Rogers Hall — named for Henry B. Rogers, Harvard class of 1822, who had donated \$8,000 — was used as a storehouse, then from 1894 by the Engineering School, and then, from 1901 to 1920 by the Germanic Museum. Casts and photographs were installed on the ground floor, with classes of the Department of Germanic Languages and Literatures held on the upper two floors. After serving as a shipping depot for the University Press in the 1920s, it was torn down in 1933, and replaced by a fire station.

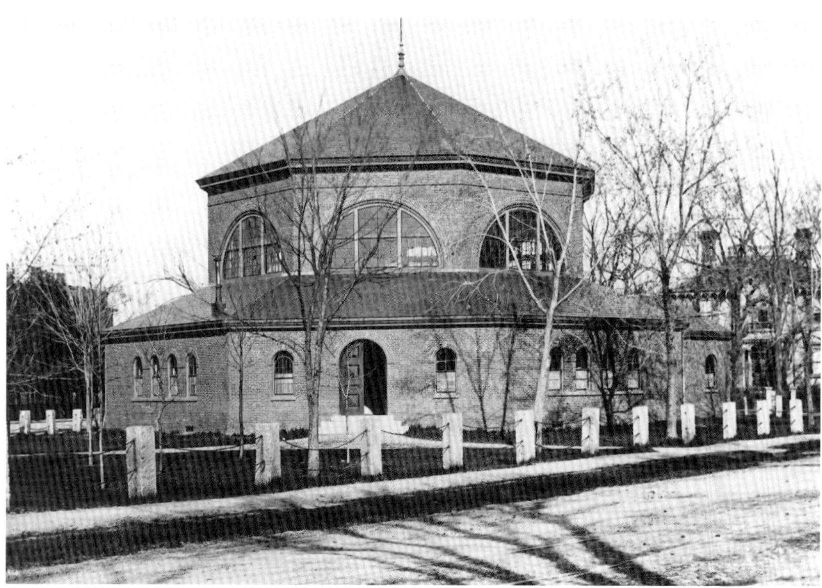

Rogers Hall, built as a gymnasium in 1859

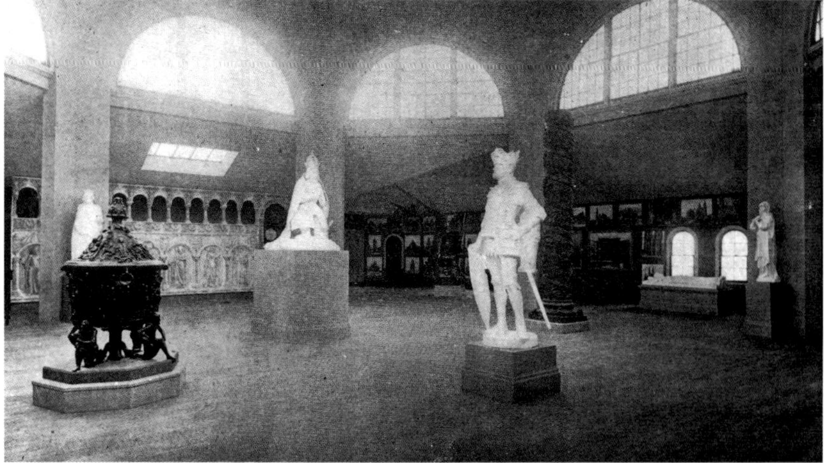

Untinted plaster casts displayed in Rogers Hall from 1903–16

Two Unrealized Proposals

G. Howard Walker proposal

The architect G. Howard Walker (1857–1936), a member of the Germanic Museum's board of directors, had in 1901 offered to make a proposal for the transformation of Rogers Hall, with its ground plan resembling a Romanesque baptisterium, into a "simply ideal receptacle of prevailingly medieval monuments" (as Francke wrote to Harvard President Eliot on June 2, 1901). In 1903, however, Walker made an altogether more ambitious proposal, now known only through the illustration and description in the Boston Sunday Journal, *January 25, 1903, reprinted here.*

In its finality of conception, with the immense wings containing art illustration of the Germanic, Slavic and Romance races, with their nine or ten sub-divisions, this great art institution will exceed all New World efforts.

As a Germanic art museum the first part to be built will be an entirely new idea for this country, though the Old World has museums devoted to distinctive racial divisions. Appropriate to this distinctive idea, the exterior architecture of each racial division will be characteristic of the art exhibit within. So the Germanic structure, to be built first, will have an outer appearance indicating that Germanic art is contained within. …

Architect G. Howard Walker says of the intended structure: "… As each wing is erected, it is proposed to make slight changes in the details of the windows, gables and entrances, which will indicate to an extent the change and variety of the work contained in the rooms within, for instance, the main facade and centre roof and dormers over the large hall have the distinct German detail of the Schloss at Heidelberg — one of the gables, the round arched windows of Romanesque work, indicating the change to the Romance Museum in this direction, another the stepped gables of the Fleisch Hall at Harlem, indicating the Flemish court, etc. …"

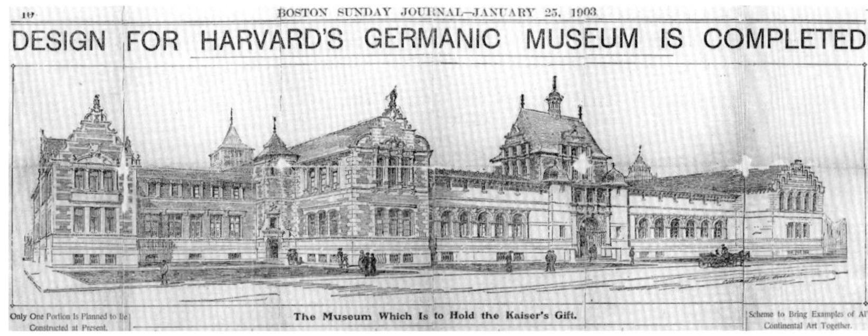

G. Howard Walker, sketch of proposed new Germanic Museum, 1903

Warren and Smith proposal

By 1908, a slightly different scheme was being suggested, designed by the Boston architectural firm of Warren and Smith and illustrated in the 1908 edition of Francke's Museum Handbook *(below).*

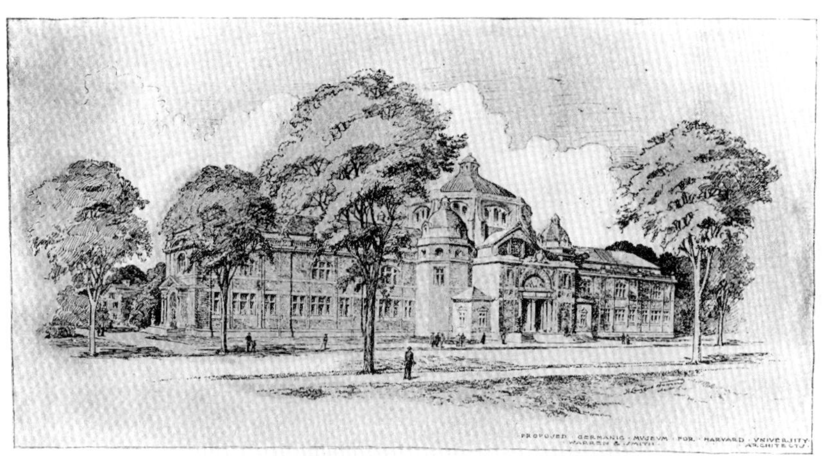

PERSPECTIVE OF A PROPOSED BUILDING FOR THE GERMANIC MUSEUM

Warren and Smith, Architects, sketch of proposed new Germanic Museum, 1908

Adolphus Busch Hall

Adolphus Busch wanted a German architect for the building for which he contributed money, and contact was made with the Dresden architect, German Bestelmeyer (1874–1942). The following two texts are both by Bestelmeyer, the first from a letter to Francke of March 29, 1910, after seeing the Warren and Smith scheme of 1908, and the second a statement elucidating his designs for the building, dated March 10, 1911. Both were originally written in German.

Bestelmeyer to Francke, 1910

… It is now more or less clear to me what a great meaning the museum will have for German culture in America, and I hope that perhaps something more original can be designed than the sketched proposal in the 1908 Handbook. … I think that the entire building must be developed out from its inner intended purpose: one must be able to see at first glance that the building can only be a "Germanic Museum," that it could not serve to house other kinds of collections; thus the exterior must obviously seek, through true monumentality, to do justice to the noble and elevated significance of the museum. In any case, I will undertake the solution of the national task with enthusiastic seriousness.…

Bestelmeyer on building design, 1911

The building is in the form of a ⌐ between Kirkland Street, Frisbie Place, and Divinity Avenue.

From each of these streets the building is set back, on an average, ten feet; only the lower parts of the structure border close to the street.

From an artistic standpoint it is very important to move these lower parts of the structure close to the street. In connection with the front parts of the building, the garden walls, and the garden itself, the building will rise from its surroundings to form an artistic group; without the projections of the outside steps the general impression would be much more subdued. The open grounds near the site and the beautiful trees absolutely demand such a conception of the architectural mass.

The ground plan is divided into a front structure, the Romanesque room, the Gothic room, and the Renaissance hall. Smaller rooms are secured partly by wings, partly by nichelike constructions and by upper stories or galleries. It is necessary to have at one's disposal rooms of as many shapes as possible for the exhibition of objects. The plan tries to carry out this idea, so that every specimen can be set up in this way or in a similar way and in proper relation to the room, as is the case with the original object.…

Concerning the form of the Museum externally and internally the following is to be said:

An adherence to one definite style I should regard as incorrect, since the purpose of the Museum is the presentation of all the epochs of German culture.

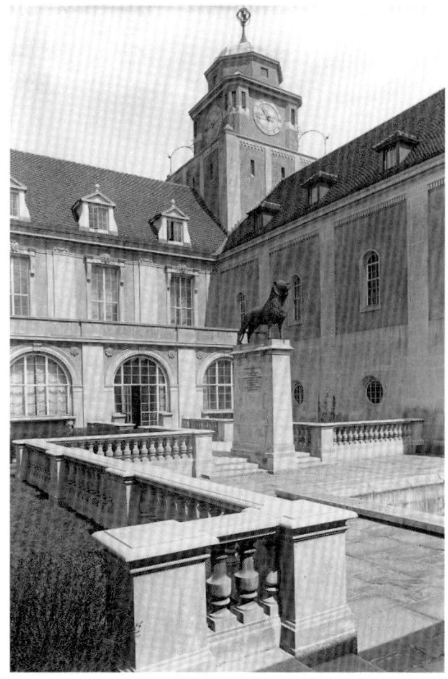

Adolphus Busch Hall, second home of the Germanic Museum: courtyard with replica of Brunswick Lion, ca. 1925

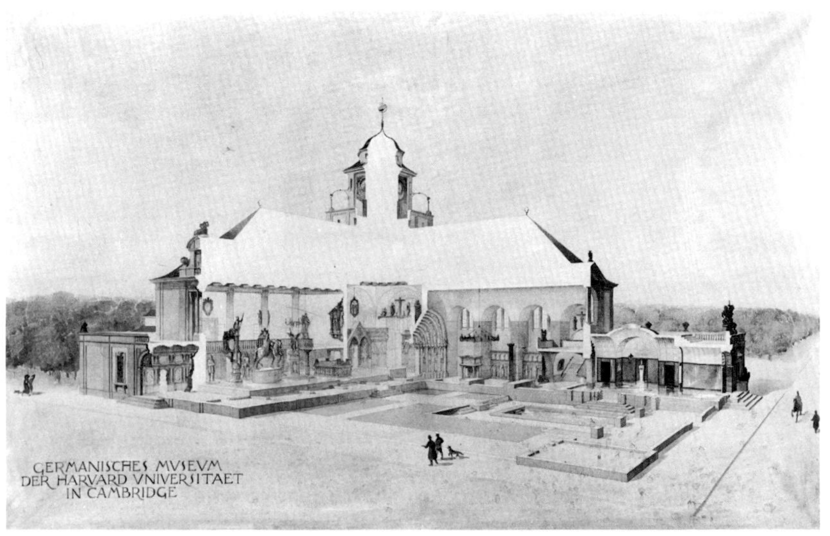

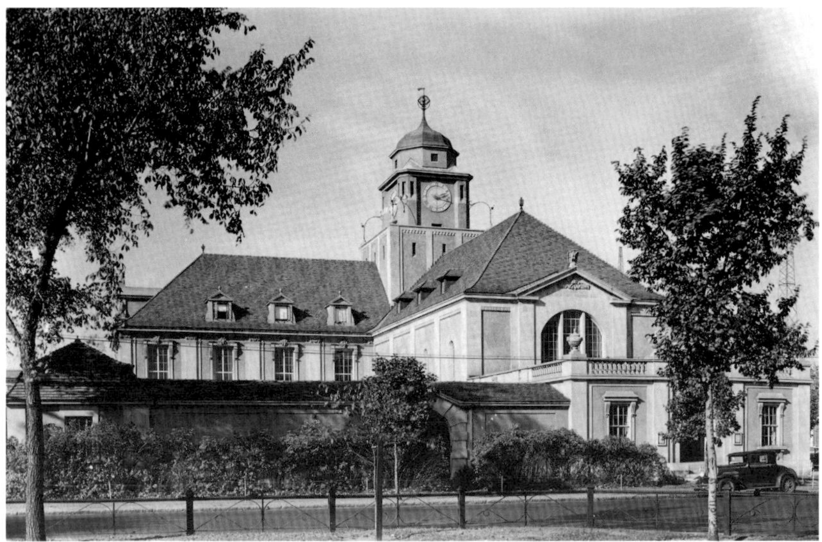

Top: *German Bestelmeyer, Sections of Adolphus Busch Hall indicating position of plaster casts, 1912*

Center: *Adolphus Busch Hall, exterior*

Right: *Adolphus Busch Hall, interior galleries, 1985*

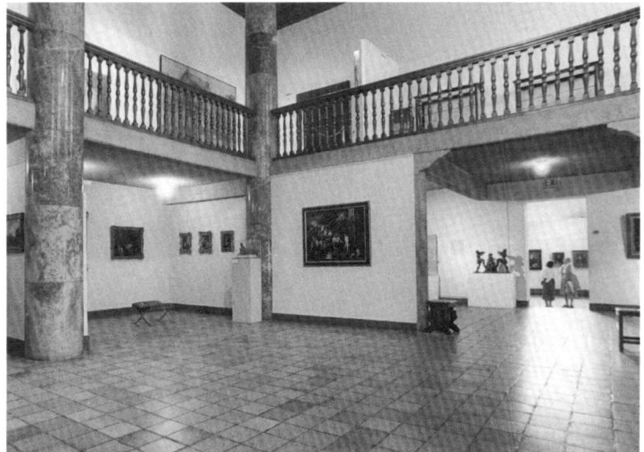

Inside, in the case of the individual rooms, a comprehensive effect is to be aimed at through the form, consequently through a certain neutrality.

The spatial and form development should indicate only the fundamental tone of the artistic epoch in question; the character of the Gothic and Romanesque will then be made clear by the arrangement of the objects themselves. To make easy this effect, the rooms must be kept simple and unadorned.

This idea must be represented also on the outside. The structure should, in its general appearance, be a symbol of the development of German culture. Solidity in the different styles is to be attained by means of the massive tower rising from the centre; it represents in itself a typical monument of the culture of German cities.

The whole structure, excluding the lower transept, the tower, and the cellar, but including all other parts of the building, contains 306,470 cubic feet. It is difficult, in such a structure, to keep exactly within the [specified] 300,000 cubic feet; to reduce the height on account of the slight excess I regard as inadvisable because of the high specimens in the exhibit and because of uniform effect of the structure ...

As material for the outside, brick is suggested with a sparing use of rough stone. In the interior, plaster is utilized with the exception of constructive and aesthetically important parts of the structure like pillars, columns, etc. which are to be made of finished stone. Tiles are suggested for the roof, copper for the top of the tower and for the garden pavilion. Stone or tile floors would have the most beautiful effect ...

Werner Otto Hall

Despite its considerable architectural charm and historical importance, Adolphus Busch Hall was never an optimum space for the preservation, display, and study of original works of art, especially of the modern period. The building was expensive to operate, lacked proper storage space, climate control, and access, and was distant from the museum-related teaching, planning, and scholarship taking place in the Fogg and Sackler Museums. This combination of factors threatened to undermine the intellectual and organizational vitality of the museum. It was decided in 1986 to aim for the construction of a new building for the Busch-Reisinger collections adjacent and attached to the Fogg. With the move of the collections out of Adolphus Busch Hall in 1987 to temporary quarters in the Fogg, the planning and fund-raising for this new structure began in earnest. In place of an official groundbreaking ceremony in late 1989, when Gwathmey Siegel & Associates of New York had finished the designs, and sufficient funds were assembled, the museum published a richly illustrated booklet with information about the plans, a list of donors, and other information. The following two texts — the first by the architect, Charles Gwathmey; the second by Peter Nisbet, curator of the museum — are taken from that booklet.

Statement by the Architect

The task of designing Werner Otto Hall for the new Busch-Reisinger Museum is a challenging formal and theoretical architectural problem. While the new building will be attached to a traditional structure, the Fogg Art Museum, it is also adjacent to Le Corbusier's modern masterpiece, the Carpenter Center, and must mediate this

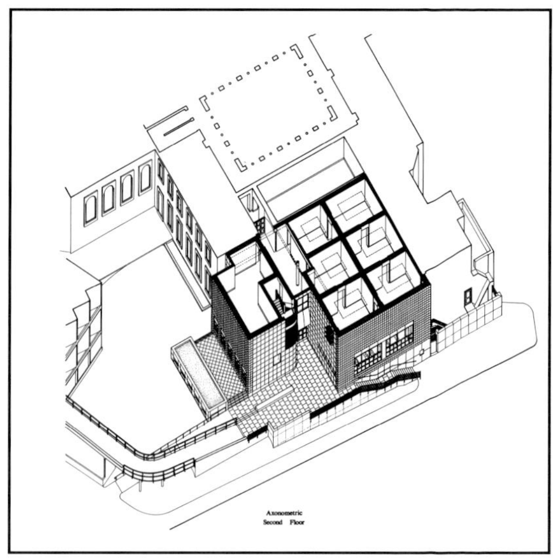

Second floor: axonometric. The new galleries will accommodate the Busch-Reisinger Museum collection. Six skylit galleries (2,800 square feet) are for the permanent collection, concentrating on art from 1880 to the present. Another gallery with natural light excluded (1,000 square feet) is for temporary exhibitions. The stair leads up to the study-storage room on the third floor. The hallway extending from the vestibule to a seating area looking out onto Prescott Street contains 500 square feet of display space.

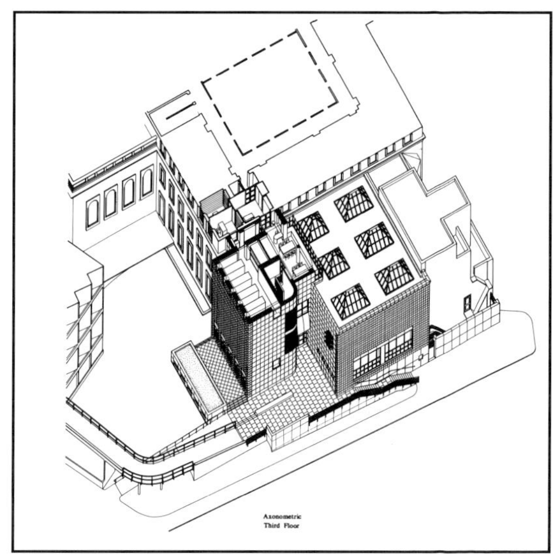

Third floor: axonometric. This level contains ample new storage and study space for the museum's holdings of works on paper, twentieth-century design and decorative arts, and archival collections. The study room will have two large work tables and appropriate north light from a generous window. The museum's curatorial offices are located adjacent to these rooms.

dual context. As an urban infill, the new building also addresses existing streetscape and scale relationships. Finally, the client requires that the building have a presence and identity of its own, distinct from the Fogg Art Museum.

The program calls for the building to house the new exhibition galleries and study-storage room for the Busch-Reisinger Museum collection, as well as parts of the Fine Arts Library relocated from the Fogg.

The solution expands on the formal architectural organization of the Fogg Art Museum. One side of the existing Fogg courtyard's peripheral circulation is extended into the new building and becomes the connection between the two major massing elements of the design. To the north are the major spaces: on the ground floor, the library reading room; on the second floor, the permanent collection galleries. These are organized in a two-story element which extends the central axis of the Fogg out to Prescott Street, and presents the new building's primary façade. To the south are the support and smaller scale spaces: on the ground floor, the library staff offices; on the second floor, the temporary exhibition gallery; and on the third floor, the study-storage room. These spaces are organized in a three-story element which is set back from the street and turns to address the Carpenter Center.

The building massing presents two simultaneous formal compositions. As a reflection of the interior organization, it can be read as two, interlocked, metal-paneled volumes, each faced with limestone on its primary façade. As well, the building's singular identity is reflected as one limestone-clad volume which has been carved away at the corner to create the plaza and reveal an "inner surface" of metal panels. From either point of view, the building addresses two important issues: the reinforcement of the street edge in the context of existing building façades and the completion of the orthogonal site framework in which the Carpenter Center is located.

The solution also resolves Le Corbusier's compelling site circulation idea. The Carpenter Center ramp, which was intended to preserve an earlier public walkway through the middle of the block, ended in the Fogg's rear yard without a connection to the Prescott Street sidewalk. The proposed design will extend the ramp onto a new library entrance plaza, from which one can descend a new exterior stair to the street.

The exterior materials will be warm gray porcelain metal panels, honed Indiana limestone, and flame-finished, gray-green granite. This color and texture palette will establish an independent graphic image for the building and is intended to mediate the monolithic scale of the concrete Carpenter Center on the one hand, and the brick and limestone of the Fogg and diamond shingles of its Naumburg wing on the other.

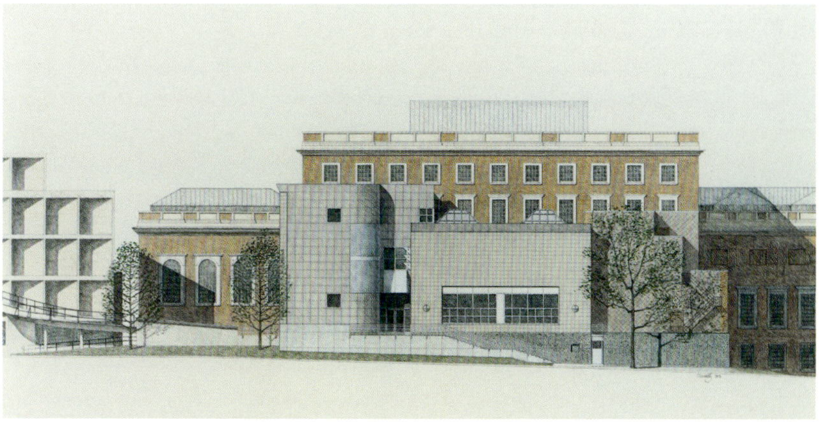

Werner Otto Hall, east elevation.

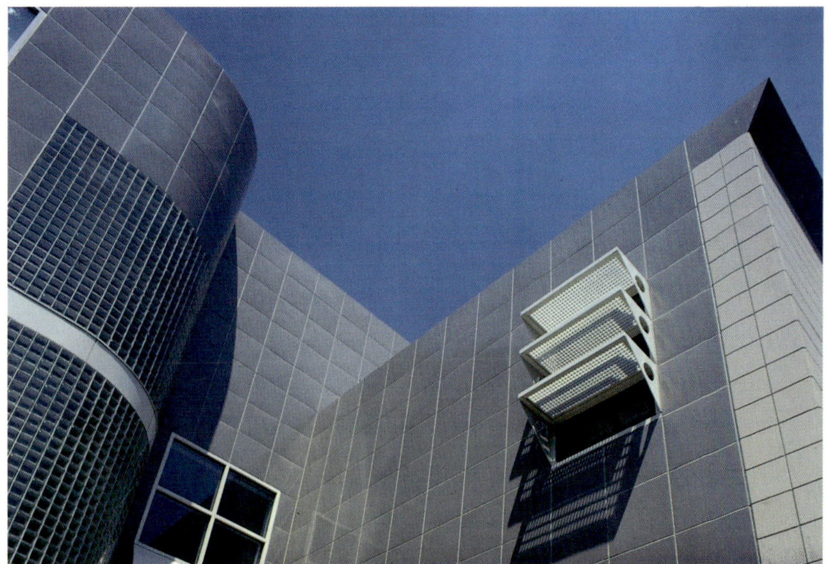

An exterior view of Werner Otto Hall showing windows on stairwell, entrance lobby, and galleries.

We believe one must understand architectural history in terms of pervasive principles rather than simply in terms of style or image. In this regard, history is a continuous exchange between old and new which is more profoundly enriched through dialogue and interpretation rather than through imitation.

Art, Accessibility, Architecture

With this intelligent and elegant building, the Busch-Reisinger Museum will have an appropriate forum in which to promote knowledge, understanding, and enjoyment of the arts of Central and Northern Europe.

The Museum has now reached the logical conclusion of a process begun in 1930, when it began to collect original works of art as its prime focus. Original works of art make substantial demands on their environment and on their publics. Our new building will go a long way towards satisfying many of those demands.

Through the sensitivity of the architects, the generosity of friends on both sides of the Atlantic, and the patient pragmatism of Harvard colleagues, these original works of art will soon be able to disturb and delight, intrigue and instruct us in ways that reflect both their intrinsic standards and the University's goals.

Perhaps the real achievement of this project is improved accessibility. This is true in the important literal sense that more of our fine and diverse collection will be more readily available to more people than ever before. With the combined and well-balanced functioning of our three main spaces (the permanent collection rooms, a gallery for changing exhibitions, and a study-seminar room with art storage), the Busch-Reisinger Museum will be able, while retaining its own identity, to contribute actively to the overall mission of the Harvard University Art Museums.

Accessibility is a goal in other senses as well. The provision of climate-control and appropriate storage will ensure that these original works of art will also be accessible to future generations. And accessibility is not just a matter of physical access to objects: it implies the best possible conditions for approaching and understanding the art.

With our new building linked to the Fogg Art Museum, the arts of German-speaking Europe will no longer suffer artificial and misleading isolation from other European and American traditions. Moreover, the provision of spaces for teaching and research, notably in the accommodation of a larger reading room and other valuable improvements to Harvard's Fine Arts Library, will also enhance the study of our collections.

More generally, this building will surely promote understanding by subtly encouraging not only careful and accurate looking under conditions which can reveal the art's full visual complexity, but also careful and accurate thinking about that experience. In other words, the building's spatial logic and aesthetic precision will, we hope, reinforce the values of critical analysis and reflection.

That all this will be possible with a building that so well fulfills urbanistic and other architectural responsibilities, is little short of exhilarating.

Art before 1880

Reproductions

Although no longer a primary focus of the museum, the collection of reproductions formed by Francke (and continued for a few years by Kuhn after 1930) is still an important and noteworthy part of the museum's responsibilities. By no means confined simply to plaster casts of sculpture and architectural elements, this collection represents a valuable teaching resource and a major achievement in its own right.

Of the original ninety-six plaster casts acquired between 1902 and 1939 (though predominantly in 1903 through the personal gift of the German emperor), about two-thirds are still in the collection. These include casts of monumental architectural stonework, like the Golden Portal of the Marienkirche in Freiberg (Saxony), the Rood Screen from the Naumburg Cathedral, and a Renaissance doorway from the Hirschvogel House in Nuremberg (the original was destroyed in World War II) by the important sculptor Peter Flötner; copies of large bronze castings like the cathedral doors of Augsburg and, from Hildesheim, the cathedral doors, baptismal font, and Bernward Column; freestanding sculptures from niches in the cathedrals of Strasbourg, Naumburg, and Bamberg; and a cast of the Kensington (Minnesota) Rune Stone, now generally considered to be a forgery. All the casts were tinted after acquisition to resemble the materials of the originals. Among the casts deaccessioned from the collection over the years are such major cathedral monuments as the Tomb of St. Sebald in Nuremberg by Peter Vischer and the Bishop's Seat from Ulm by Jörg Syrlin; full-scale plaster models of armed Frankish and Roman warriors and a scale model fifth-century Scandinavian boat; and reliefs from Trajan's Column in Rome.

Prompted by the emperor's gift, a group of Berlin citizens arranged in 1903 for the manufacture and donation of a collection of fifty-five electroplated copies of German gilt silver originals from the fifteenth to eighteenth centuries, housed in museums throughout Europe.

Other important items within this category include 141 electroplate copies of plaques of religious and mythological subjects by Flötner and others from the Basel Museum; ten metal reproductions of seventh-century Merovingian brooches

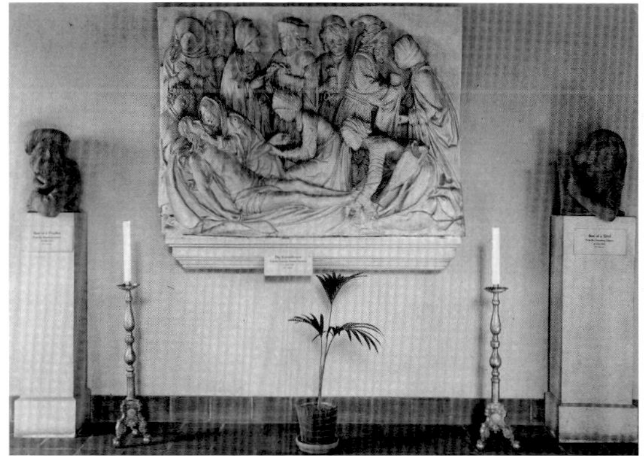

Adam Krafft (1450/60–1507), Entombment (from the Nuremberg Stations of the Cross). Plaster cast. Gift, BR30.19. This cast is flanked by heads of an old man and a girl (both 1464) by Nikolaus Gerhaert, active 1460–86; the originals, now destroyed, were in the chancellery at Strasbourg. BR30.20, 21.

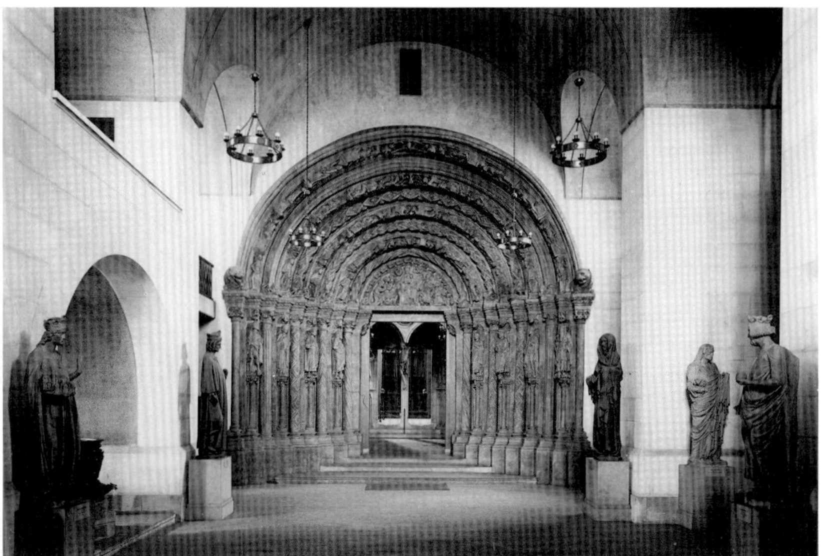

German, 12th century, Golden Portal of the Marienkirche in Freiberg, Saxony. Plaster cast. Gift, BR30.38.

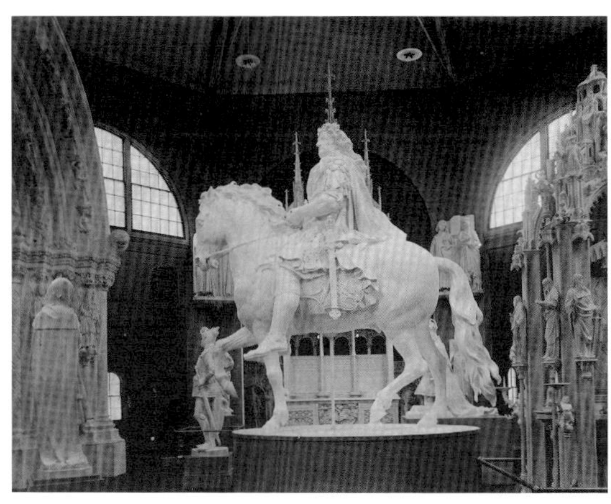

Interior of Rogers Hall with plaster cast of the Great Elector by Andreas Schlüter (1664–1714), original sculpture completed 1698–1703.

from Ulm; and an electroplated copy of a sixteenth-century German sword. Incorporated into the architectural ensemble of Adolphus Busch Hall and its courtyard were a full-size cast of the Lion outside the Ducal Palace in Brunswick (1166) and copies of six fifteenth-century Austrian windows, installed in the apse of Adolphus Busch Hall, the latter now deaccessioned.

Acquired in 1922 from F.W. Miller, the Rhode Island artist who had executed the tinting of the plaster casts, were ninety-eight reproductions of ivories comprising late Roman, Byzantine, and German book covers, plaques, caskets, and statuettes from the third to the fifteenth centuries.

An important though sometimes overlooked part of the collection of copies are over six hundred photographs, posters, and reproductions of major paintings, drawings, and prints. Some of the earliest known purchases by Kuhn included reproductions of the *Red Horses* by Franz Marc (then in Essen, now on long-term loan to the Busch-Reisinger and to the Cincinnati Art Museum); Runge's *Playing Children* (Hamburg); Cuyp's *The Ford* (Vienna); and Dürer's *Self-Portrait* (Munich). Originally part of a study collection, including some that circulated in traveling exhibitions, this group grew to include duplicates which were framed and lent out to individuals. Almost all have since been transferred to library study collections.

Francke was quite proud of his collection. After a trip to Germany in 1922, he wrote in his annual report: "Most gratifying was the friendly interest in our museum shown to me by all museum authorities in Germany. The heads of the various 'Kunsthistorische Institute' [sic] connected with universities, whom I met, were unanimous in taking a kind of jealous pride in the fact that our collection of casts offers a better opportunity for the study of the development of German sculpture in its chief phases than any similar institution in Germany. Just now the Deutsches Museum at Berlin is undertaking to build up a collection of casts of similar scope, and the Germanisches Nationalmuseum at Nürnberg is considering the same step — surely an encouragement for us to continue on the way we entered upon twenty-five years ago."

Not all people agreed, however, that only reproductions should comprise the collection. A flyer of around 1902 announcing the formation of the Germanic Museum Association, with Carl Schurz as president, discussed "models and reproductions" but added that "[f]rom the very beginning, however, it is proposed to make an effort to secure originals also; weapons and costumes, implements and utensils; engravings, to illustrate the art of the engraver, or to show the customs of a period; books illustrating the history of printing; paintings, sculptures, and carvings of real value, artistically or historically." Considering the present state of the museum, this program can be seen as prophetic: it could apply to the collection of twentieth-century art and design (though the museum has yet to acquire any weapons, modern or otherwise).

Medieval, Renaissance, and Baroque Art

With the architecture of Adolphus Busch Hall and the museum's collection of reproductions focused on styles before 1700, it was surely natural in 1930 for Kuhn to acquire original works from this period. Early accessions included a Thuringian

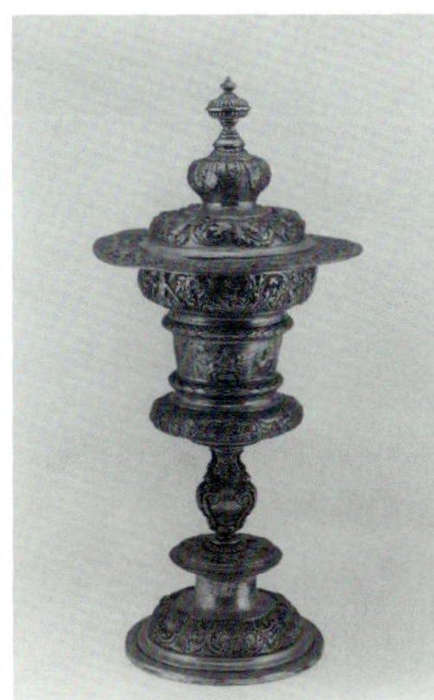

Augsburg School, 16th century, Goblet of the Butchers' Guild. *Electrotype reproduction of an original in the Bavarian National Museum, Munich, h. 43.2 cm. Gift of Citizens of Berlin, BR03.39.*

altarpiece of 1516 (1932), a Westphalian Crucifix panel (1933), a 1506 print by Cranach, and examples of sixteenth-century decorative arts. However, as with other aspects of Kuhn's ambitions, serious and systematic expansion of the holdings from these earlier centuries had to wait for the stabilization of the museum's finances around 1950 and, more particularly, for a conscious shift of emphasis away from the twentieth-century collections. In his annual report for 1954–55, Kuhn averred that the museum could turn its attention to other areas, notably the nineteenth century (a goal never satisfactorily achieved, as described below), and to the medieval, Renaissance, and baroque periods.

"The work of these epochs are widely scattered [in America], … and those examples in the public collections of Greater Boston can give our students only a vague and very incomplete impression of the character and significance of the visual arts of these periods. Such objects are also scarce and often extremely costly, but by the careful husbanding of present resources and through the generosity of future donors, it is possible that they may be acquired."

Even before writing this programmatic statement, Kuhn had acquired some significant pieces: in 1949, a dramatic Danube School sculpture of St. Michael dating around 1510–20, and in 1951, a fine soapstone relief by Flötner and important sixteenth-century stained glass (a gift of Henry P. McIlhenny). Towards the

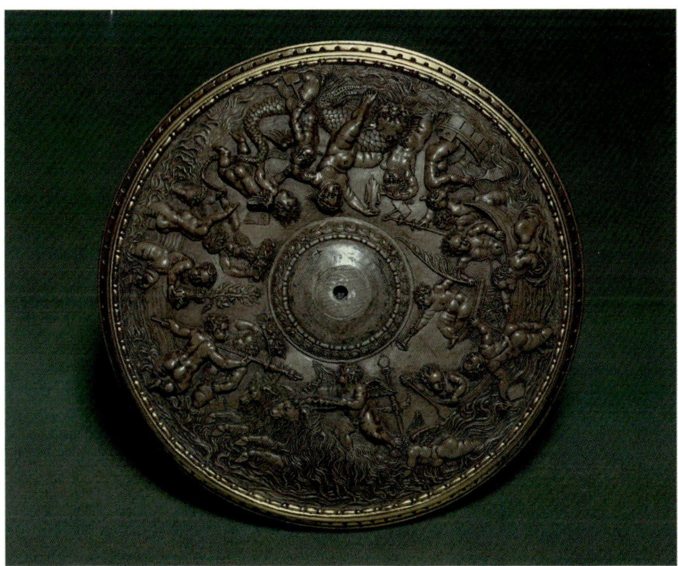

Peter Flötner (1485–1546), Triumph of a Sea-Goddess, *ca. 1530. Soapstone, diam. 17.5 cm. Association Fund, BR51.213.*

end of the 1950s acquisitions increased, encouraged by Walter Davis's endowment of a fund named for Antonia Paepcke DuBrul (Radcliffe '57). From the sixteenth century, decorative arts (an Augsburg silver tankard, brass bowls, Flemish candlesticks, stove tiles, etc.), half a dozen wood sculptures, and other works entered the collections. A moving Austrian *Pietà* of about 1420, bought in 1959, was nicely matched four years later with the purchase of a well-preserved *Schoene Madonna* of approximately the same date. Fifteenth-century works in general were apparently a priority for Kuhn in the last decade of his curatorship, with many sculptures and objects from this era (especially from the Upper Rhine, South Germany, and Austria) entering the collections, though the sixteenth and seventeenth centuries were by no means neglected. Kuhn was also able to deepen the holdings in this area by drawing on long-term loans and transfers from the Fogg's collections (notably in sculpture).

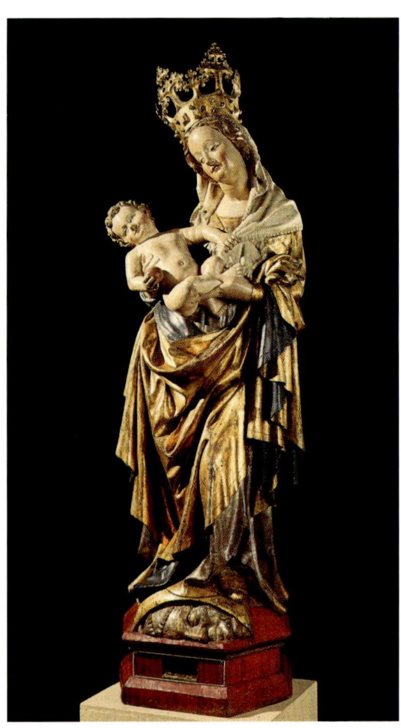

Tyrolean, 15th century, **Madonna and Child, ca. 1430. Polychromed wood, h. 155 cm. Anonymous funds, BR63.2.**

Given Kuhn's commitment to building up these aspects of the collection, it was only fitting that the work of art the museum acquired in honor of his retirement in 1968 was not a twentieth-century piece (the field in which Kuhn had made the museum's reputation), but a fine example of the German Renaissance, Riemenschneider's 1510 *St. Anthony Abbot*. Similarly, gifts received on this occasion were also from the early sixteenth century: a fine drawing by Amman (from Mr. and Mrs. Peter Wick), an anonymous 1516 drawing of St. Jerome (from

Upper Rhenish, 17th century, **Death with left hand raised; Death with outstretched right arm, 1600–1650. Lindenwood, h. 25.7 and 27 cm. Association Fund, BR59.32, BR59.33.**

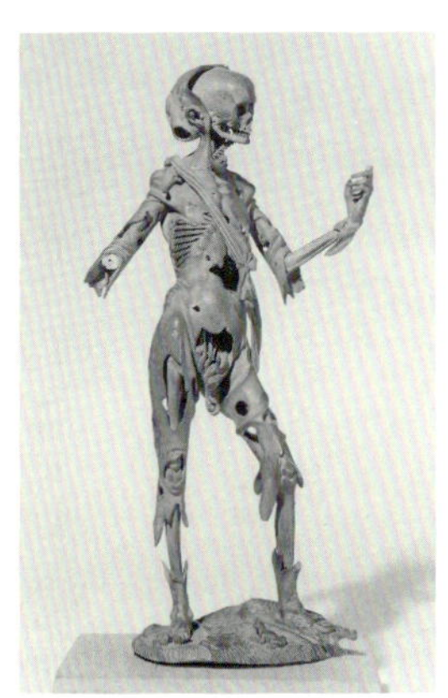
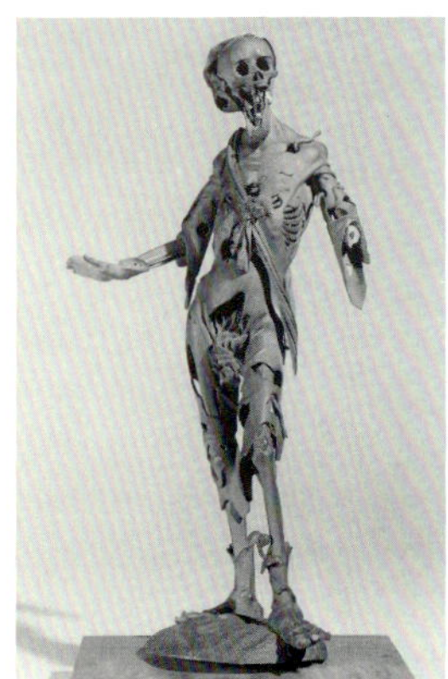

Philip Hofer), and a 1508 van Leyden engraving (from Mr. and Mrs. William Coe). Since then, it must be said that the pre-1700 collections have not been expanded noticeably, with the surprising exception of sixteenth-century painting.

As a rule, Kuhn had not concentrated on painting, relying instead on exhibiting several of the Fogg's very fine works from this period. Many of the Fogg paintings were in fact transferred in the 1960s to the collection of the Busch-Reisinger, which in turn gave up a large majority of its collection of prints to the Fogg. (These paintings are not enumerated here since the exchange was reversed in 1990 as part of the refinement

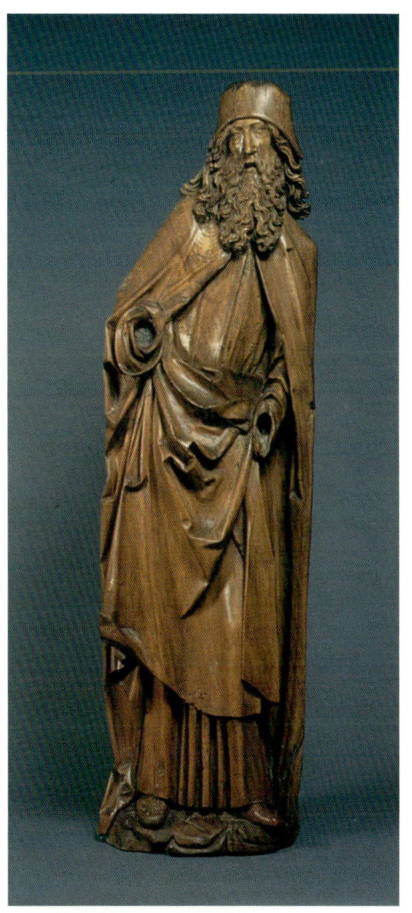

Tilman Riemenschneider (c. 1450–1531), St. Anthony Abbot, ca. 1510. Lindenwood, h. 117.5 cm. Anonymous fund and special gifts from the friends of Charles L. Kuhn, BR69.214.

Hans von Aachen (1552–1616), Venus and Adonis, ca. 1574–88. Oil, 65.4 x 93.3 cm. The Friends of the Busch-Reisinger Museum and anonymous funds, BR77.11.

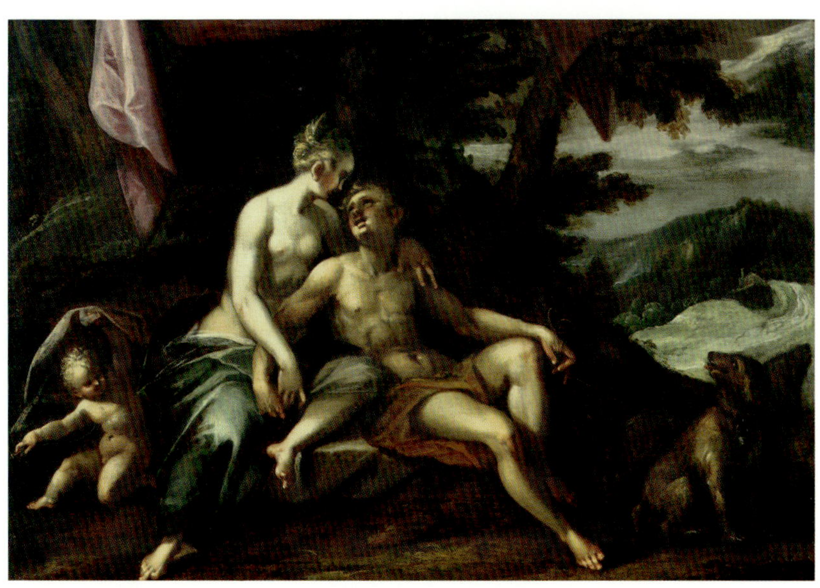

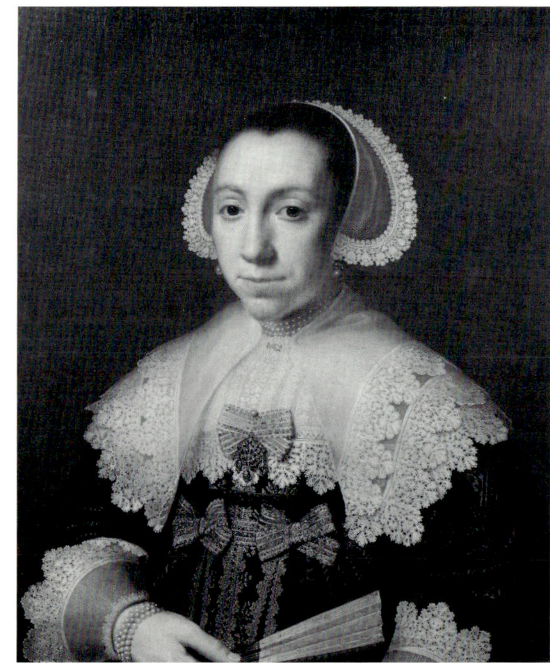

Dirck Dircksz. van Santvoort (1610/11–1680), Elisabet de St. Gilles, betrothed to N. van Lier, ca. 1635. Oil on panel, 63.5 x 52 cm. Bequest of Hetty L. Shuman Kuhn, 1990.77.

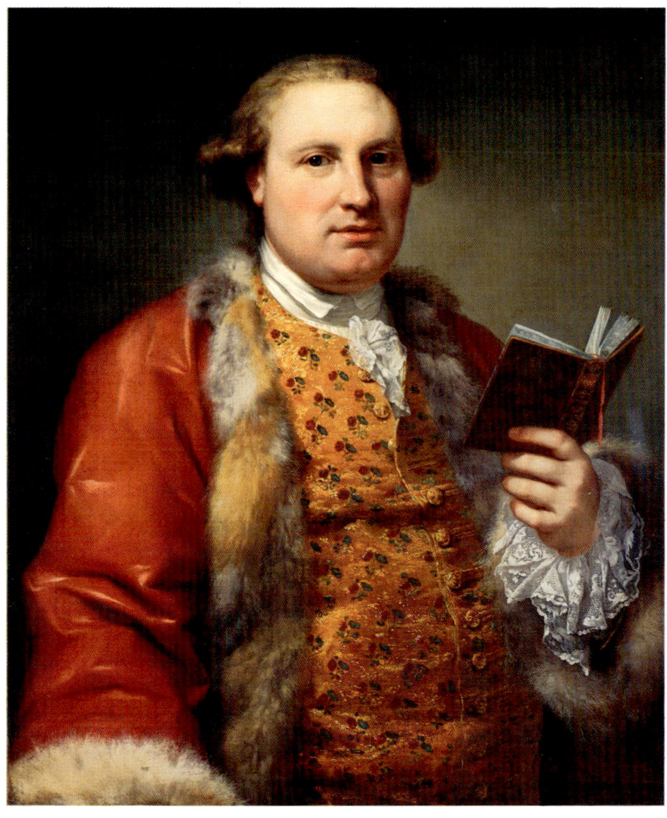

Anton von Maron (1733–1808), Portrait of Archibald Menzies, 1763. Oil, 76.2 x 63.5 cm. Gift of Robert Rantoul Endicott, BR57.147.

and reinforcement of the Busch-Reisinger's mission.) Beyond this, Kuhn added only about a dozen paintings from the fifteenth to the seventeenth centuries, all relatively minor study pieces.

The purchase in 1977 of von Aachen's mannerist *Venus and Adonis* has been complemented by 1981 gifts from Mr. and Mrs. John Steiner of a 1530 Nuremberg portrait and from Mr. Mortimer Brandt of *Hercules and Cerberus*, attributed to Uffenbach, and by the purchase in 1985 of Schwarz's 1580 *Adoration of the Shepherds*, acquired with funds provided by Dr. Alfred Bader. (In 1979 Mrs. Steiner also gave an interesting, unattributed South German watercolor of the *Last Judgment* from the early seventeenth century.) With important works such as these and the more important of Kuhn's acquisitions, the Busch-Reisinger effectively strengthens the representation of Northern European art from earlier centuries in the galleries of the Fogg.

The Eighteenth and Early Nineteenth Centuries

Already in 1936 Kuhn wrote of the eighteenth century as "one of the most interesting periods in the history of German art." Thirty years later this era had become the best represented in the Busch-Reisinger's collections (excepting the twentieth), with a delicately balanced selection of fine works, including sculpture, paintings, works on paper, and decorative arts.

The outlines of this broad overview of the German rococo were already set in Kuhn's first years. The 1936 purchase of Elliger's *Venus and Mars* went along with the gift of a Bavarian polychromed *Head of an Angel*, two Nymphenburg porcelain figurines (the nucleus of a much larger collection, described below), and

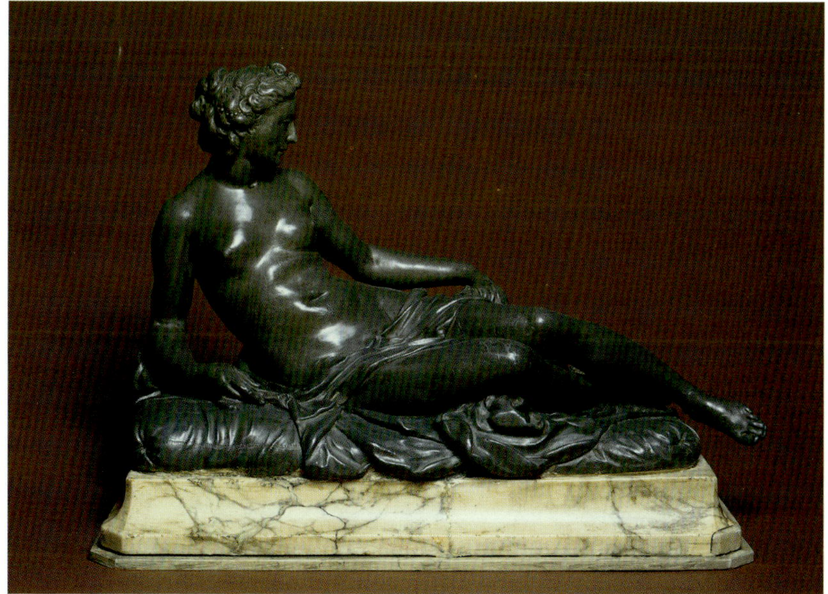

Georg Raphael Donner (1693–1741), Reclining Nymph, *ca. 1739. Lead statuette on marble base, h. 25.4 cm. Association Fund, BR64.7.*

prints by Chodowiecki (subsequently deaccessioned, though this Berlin chronicler of middle-class genre is still well represented through the 1941 gift of over thirty-five prints). It was also in 1941 that Kuhn purchased *The Four Seasons*, four magnificent late eighteenth-century garden statues attributed to Johann Joachim Günther, though these were sold to the Fogg in 1952.

As in other areas of the collection, the late 1950s saw a rapidly increasing rate of acquisitions of eighteenth-century material. Paintings by Pesne (a portrait of a general), Zick (*The Daughter of Jairus*), Tischbein (two studies for a series of large-scale works on the theme of Cleopatra), and Rottmeyr (a *Deposition*) were purchased between 1956 and 1964, joining gifts over these same eight years of paintings by von Maron (*Portrait of Archibald Menzies*, from Ralph Rantoul Endicott, Harvard '26), von Kobell (a 1762 landscape from Kuhn himself) and Zeller (a portrait of a nobleman).

Sculpture was, as always, a special focus for the Busch-Reisinger. Among the numerous acquisitions of three-dimensional work from this period, religious pieces are especially notable. Parts of an over-life-size Austrian altarpiece (*St. Augustine* and *St. Ambrose*), Guggenbichler's splendid *Holy Family* altarpiece, and a Viennese *Magdalen in the Desert* can stand here *pars pro toto*. Highlights of secular work include an alabaster *Judith and Holofernes*, and Donner's *Reclining Nymph* (purchased from the Fogg in 1964, as were a few other sculptures in these years), as well as the extensive collection of porcelains.

Eighteenth-Century Porcelains

The Busch-Reisinger collection of eighteenth-century German porcelains began with a few scattered purchases of figurines in the 1930s, but the majority of what can be seen as a well-rounded study collection representing each of the major eighteenth-century manufactories, as well as the diversity of iconographic themes

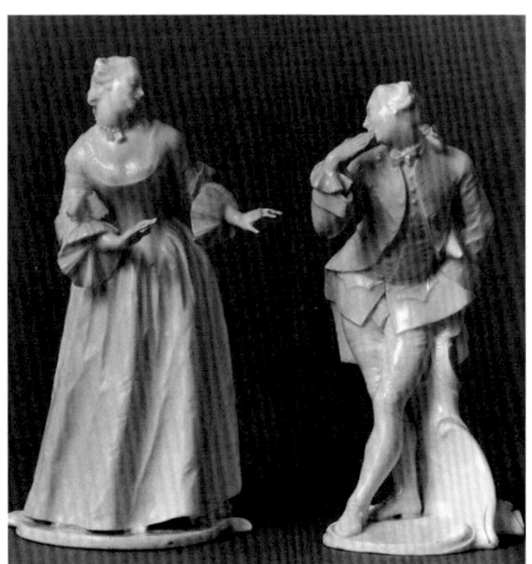

Franz Bustelli (1723–64), modeler, Nymphenburg manufacture, Isabella and Octavio, ca. 1760. Porcelain, h. 19.1 and 18.5 cm. Gift of Charles Kuhn in memory of Minnie S. Kuhn. BR33.14, BR33.15.

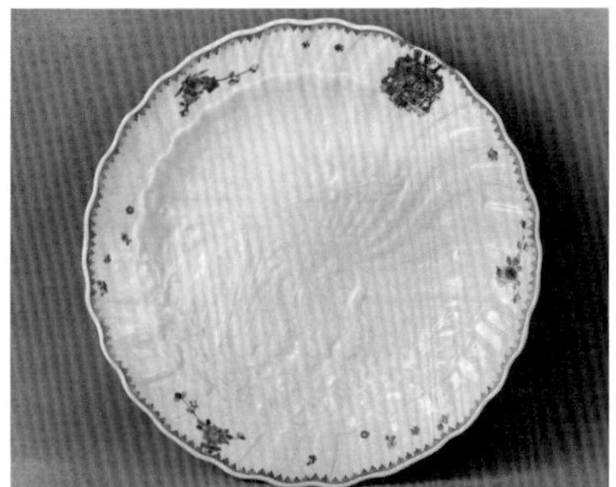

J.J. Kändler (1707–75), modeler, Meissen manufacture, Swan Service Platter, ca. 1736–1741. Porcelain, diam. 30.1 cm. Gift of Ilse Bischoff, BR59.136.

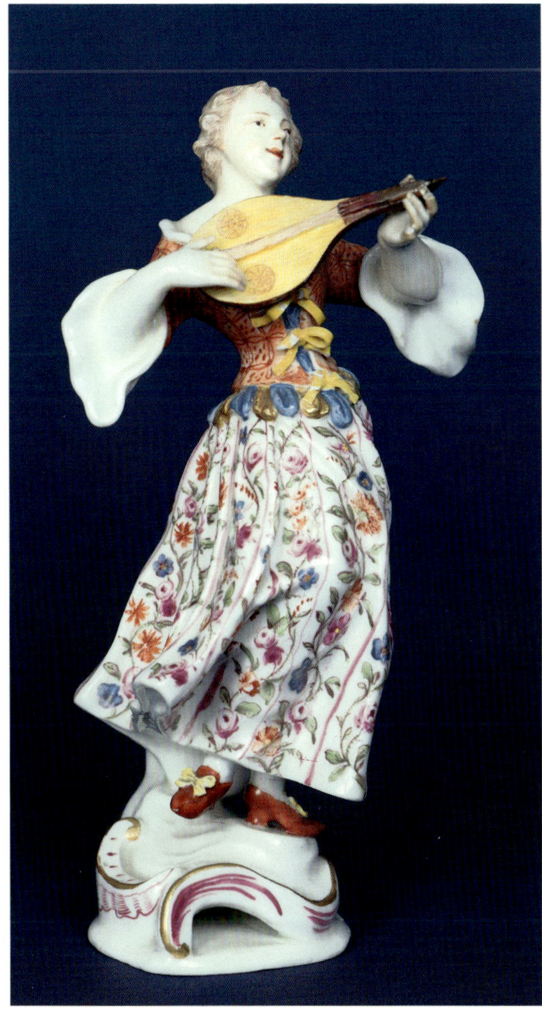

German, 18th century,
Höchst manufacture,
Mandolin Player, *ca. 1755*
Porcelain, h. 15.5 cm. Gift
of Ilse Bischoff, BR78.8.

in table services, figurines, and curiosa, was assembled beginning in the late 1950s and continued throughout the 1960s. Kuhn's programmatic interest in the decorative arts inspired, in the area of eighteenth-century porcelains, the generosity of several collectors spearheaded by a long-standing patron of the Busch-Reisinger, the painter and writer Ilse Bischoff, who had been an art student in Germany. Bischoff assisted Kuhn in obtaining numerous gifts from her sister and brother-in-law, Mr. and Mrs. H. Graves Terwilliger; the business executive Mr. Edward M. Pflueger and his wife; and Dr. Hans Syz, psychiatrist and notable collector of European and Asian porcelains now part of the Smithsonian Institution. At present the collection consists of forty-one figurines and fifty-six serving pieces.

Since Asian porcelains dominated the market prior to the founding of Meissen, it is understandable that a substantial portion of the earliest articles produced under the auspices of the Saxon court were objects of Asian pattern and design. Very appealing to the Dresden court in particular was the Japanese decorative style known as *Kakiemon*. Plates made for two very early Meissen table services designed for Augustus the Strong are represented in the Busch-Reisinger collection: the "red tiger" plate and the "yellow tiger" plate. Both bear the prestigious "Johanneum" mark, an incised and blackened inventory number indicating that a piece was originally in Augustus's personal collection. A third handsome service represented in the Busch-Reisinger collection is the famous Swan Service of 1737–42 designed by the noted Modellmeister Johann Joachim Kändler. Kändler's over two thousand-piece service designed for Heinrich von Brühl, prime minister and director of Meissen, demonstrated his facility with sculptural forms as well as his ingenious selection of iconographic motifs. In this case, two swans and two herons inhabit a marsh (in German, *Brühl*).

Kändler was also largely responsible for the widened interest in figural compositions based on the *trionfi*, or sugar sculptures, which have been common table decorations for the dessert course of a meal. His compositions included a variety of themes such as the Commedia dell'Arte, religious subjects, genre subjects, and mythological themes. Among the finest of these is the figure of Melpomene, the muse of tragedy, made for a figural series commissioned by Catherine the Great (the large "E" for Ekaterina on the back of the base identifying the figure as Melpomene indicates this).

Two of the manufactories preferred by Ilse Bischoff for their sculptural elegance were Höchst and Nymphenburg. Höchst was particularly noted for its rustic imagery as well as its peasant figurines, a few of which are present in the Busch-Reisinger collection. Nymphenburg under the modeler Franz Anton Bustelli, however, came to firmly represent the rococo with the elegant and elongated contraposto poses of figures and suitable embellishments made to the bases of the figures. The Busch-Reisinger pair of Commedia dell'Arte figurines, Octavio and Isabella, are beautifully representative of Bustelli's craft. Other smaller manufactories represented in the collection are Ansbach, Berlin, Frankenthal, Fürstenberg, Kloster Veilsdorf, and Ludwigsburg, each of which show a demonstrated affinity with the tastes set early on by Meissen.

It is surely one of the disappointments in the history of the Busch-Reisinger Museum that this strong foundation of eighteenth-century art could never be linked to the outstanding holdings of the twentieth century through a full and appropriate representation of the nineteenth. Though Kuhn repeatedly referred to the necessity of expanding this field, as one when literature and the visual arts were very closely intertwined and therefore of great interest and value in teaching the history of Germanic culture, circumstances must have conspired against the fulfillment of this dream. Had the Busch-Reisinger been able to take advantage of the relatively low prices for German and Austrian art of the nineteenth century in the 1950s (when at least one outstanding private collection of this material was amassed in Germany), the consistency of the Busch's holdings over several centuries might have argued for its continued existence as a fully autonomous museum of Germanic art. The absence of major works by Friedrich, Runge, Overbeck, Pforr, Menzel, Feuerbach, and so many others is keenly felt.

Of course, the nineteenth century is not wholly unrepresented. Indeed, the first original work of art acquired by the Busch-Reisinger (ceremonial portraits and

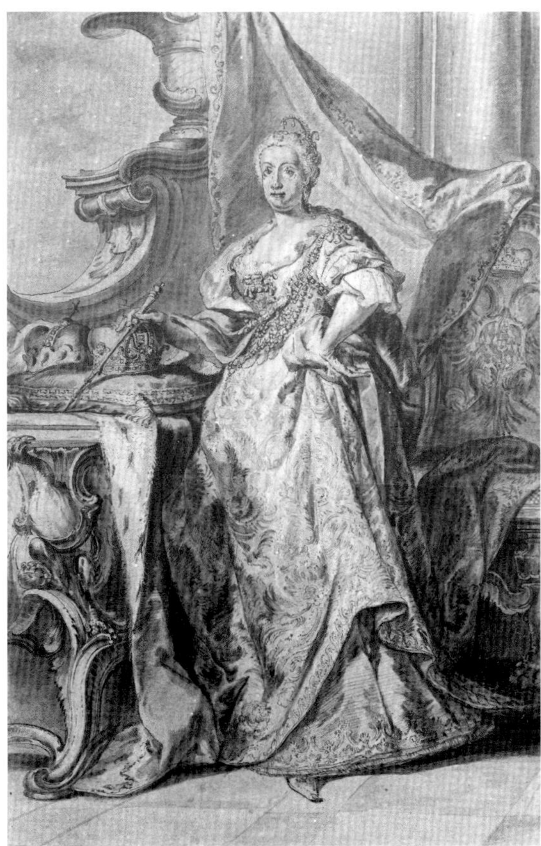

Johann Wolfgang Baumgartner (1712–61), Empress Maria Amalia. *Pen and black ink, grey wash and white gouache on blue-green antique laid paper, 36.0 x 23.1 cm. Purchase through the generosity of the Harvard Class of 1936 in appreciation of their friend and classmate, Ernst Teves, BR82.3.*

a tapestry aside) was an 1867 drawing by von Kaulbach, bequeathed in 1924. In his initial inventory in 1930, Kuhn seems to have found a set of drawn Faust illustrations (by Voltz, Kiellerup, and others, apparently a gift of Henry Ware Holland), and he soon acquired, by gift or purchase, two anonymous (but rather fine) mid-century figure studies, a battle scene by Steinle, drawings by the caricaturist Oberländer, and a set of four religious scenes by an artist of the Nazarene School.

In the field of prints Kuhn acquired illustrative sheets by Richter (in 1938, a set of eight as a gift from Mrs. Kuno Francke), and this modest foundation was supplemented in 1957 through the arrival of a substantial number of German prints of the eighteenth and early nineteenth centuries (especially the latter) as the gift of the dealer J.B. Neumann, who had played such a prominent role in introducing twentieth-century German art to the United States. In addition to fourteen further sheets by Richter, this gift included works by Achenbach, Bolt, Hagedorn, Wagenbauer, Tischbein, Schwind, and others. In the same year, Philip Hofer gave Rethel's *Hannibalzug*.

The late 1950s saw the addition of a very few further drawings, such as a Horny landscape (given by Mr. and Mrs. Reginald Phelps in 1958) and two Spitzwegs (bought in 1959). Nineteenth-century paintings and sculpture hardly fared better, with two Bavarian glass paintings acquired in 1954, and a Tyrolean

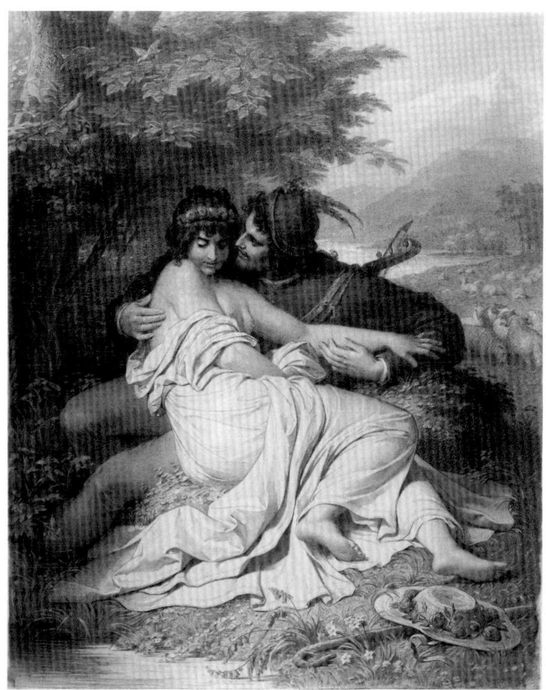

**W. von Kaulbach (1805–74),
Under the Linden Trees,
1867. Black charcoal, 149.9
x 119.4 cm. Gift of Mrs.
Herbert L. Sakerlee, BR24.1**

landscape of about 1830 by Bürkel in 1955 (from Mr. and Mrs. Lyonel Feininger).

Since Kuhn's retirement in 1968, it has not proved possible to augment these holdings in a way that might transform their character. For the eighteenth century, one painting (an anonymous portrait of a boy, acquired in 1985) and one sculpture (a wax *Madonna* from Kloster Lambach, bequeathed by Betty Bartlett McAndrew in 1986) can be mentioned. The field of eighteenth-century drawings has fared slightly better, with works by J.C.J. Friedrich (in 1970), Roos (1972), Brand (1981), Tröger, and Baumgartner (both 1982) entering the collections.

For the nineteenth century (at least for the period up to around 1880), the accession lists record a neoclassical sculpture by a member of the Schwanthaler family (*Venus and Cupid on a Dolphin*, purchased in 1970), a set of Biedermeier furnishings and pastel portraits (bequeathed by Alice Lorris in 1971), a breakfast set of Nymphenburg porcelain (given by Kuhn himself in 1978), and six pieces of so-called Berlin iron jewelry (given in 1985 by Mrs. Frank Stanton). Around 1971, a number of interesting drawings were acquired, including sheets by Birmann (as a gift of D. Thomas Bergen), Laufberger, Zimmerman, and Menta, as well as anonymous sheets given by Philip Hofer. For the print collection, works by Menzel were given to the Busch in 1971 and in 1987 (by Daniel Bell). In the areas of nineteenth-century prints and drawings, however, the holdings of the Fogg are of great importance for the student and scholar. Works by some of the great names so sorely lacking from the Busch-Reisinger's files may be found there, offering one more argument in favor of the close cooperation which can bring so much benefit to the Busch, especially in those areas where its own holdings, through circumstance or design, are not in themselves of sufficient weight to stand alone.

THE MODERN COLLECTIONS

The Busch-Reisinger Museum's modern collections are particularly strong and cohesive. The holdings of art and design from the century 1880–1980 are, in fact, sufficiently good to support the museum's status as a relatively independent institution — a separate museum-like department within the Harvard University Art Museums — especially as this is the part of the collection most actively used in teaching and research at Harvard. Otto Hall has been designed with these collections and these activities in mind.

Art and Design, 1880–1945

From the very beginning of his thirty-eight year tenure as curator, Kuhn emphasized modern art in his acquisition program. Already in 1931, he bought — with the help of his friend and colleague Edward M. M. Warburg (Harvard '30) — Barlach's monumental figure of the *Crippled Beggar*, designed for the facade of a church in Lübeck. This architectural sculpture must have been ideally suited to the large-scale plaster casts and open spaces of Adolphus Busch Hall. Indeed, the nature of these exhibition galleries may have encouraged Kuhn to make sculpture a focus of his collecting activities. Within six years, about a dozen further examples of modern German sculpture, in particular works by Kolbe, Sintenis, Belling, and Lehmbruck, had been added. The first decade (or rather, the years up to 1937, when acquisitions almost completely ceased for about ten years) also saw a concentration on prints (like sculpture, also a reproductive medium, though in this case suited to the library and study spaces of Adolphus Busch Hall). Barlach was a favorite here too, along with Kandinsky, Klee, Kollwitz, Heckel, Munch, and others. A handful of fine drawings, including works by sculptors like Kolbe and Marcks,

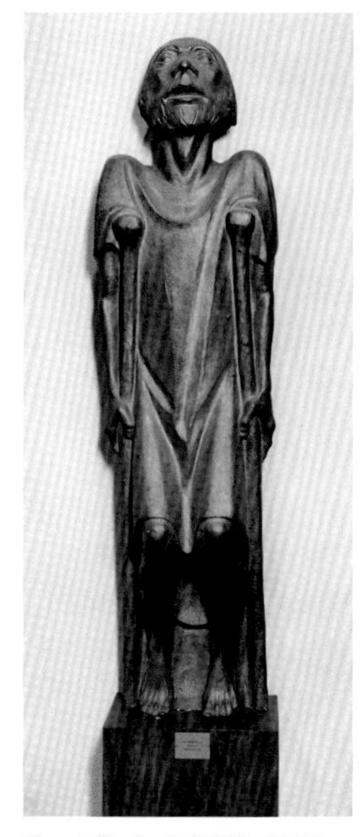

Ernst Barlach (1870–1938),
Crippled Beggar, 1930.
Terracotta, h. 221 cm.
Museum purchase, BR31.5.

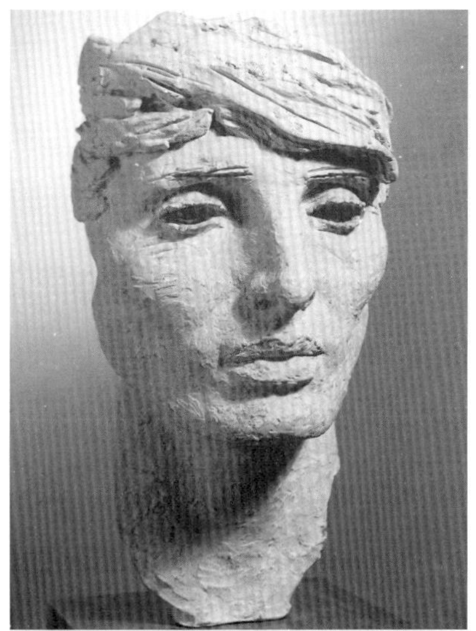

Renée Sintenis (1888–1965), **Self-Portrait,** *1931. Terracotta, h. 34.3 cm. Museum purchase, BR31.74.*

as well as Klee, Grosz, Dix, and Hofer, were also purchased or given. Kuhn traveled several times to Germany in the 1930s to find pieces, with a particularly notable trip in 1934. It is worth remembering that even then Kuhn was buying art by contemporary artists who were incurring the displeasure and active repression of the National Socialists.

These early years of collecting in the modern field also provide evidence of Kuhn's love for the decorative arts. He bought widely, adding examples of Danish modern design (by Georg Jensen), Swedish, Austrian, and Dutch glassware (in 1931 and 1933), German typography (including, as a gift of the designer, a large collection of posters and printed material by the Hamburg artist Mahlau), and much other similar material. Curiously, he bought hardly any three-dimensional work by Bauhaus artists during the 1930s.

The Second World War all but extinguished the Busch-Reisinger Museum. Not only did it call into question the institutional foundations of the museum (as recounted elsewhere in this book), it also put an effective stop to collecting activity, especially in the modern field. No modern drawings or sculpture were added between 1938 and 1948, while the print collection added only an impression of Lehmbruck's and a portfolio by George Grosz in 1942 (though the Fogg Art Museum continued its own active acquisition program of modern German prints, begun in the late 1920s). The one outstanding exception to this rather bleak picture was the 1941 purchase of the museum's first modern oil painting, Beckmann's 1927 *Self-Portrait in Tuxedo*, which the National Socialists had confiscated from the Berlin Nationalgalerie and traded abroad. For $600, Kuhn acquired one of the great paintings of the twentieth century, a work that has ever since been the museum's signature piece.

The extraordinary revitalization of the museum begun in the late 1940s enabled Kuhn to surround the Beckmann and the rest of the modern collections with an astonishing array of expressionist and abstract masterpieces. In the few years from 1949 to the late 1950s, he assembled many of the works which today define the character of the museum as a unique resource for the study and enjoyment of modern art from German-speaking Europe.

For the paintings collection in 1950 alone, Kuhn was able to purchase an important early abstract painting by Moholy-Nagy, Feininger's key *Bird Cloud*, Heckel's 1909 *Bathers* and his 1913 masterpiece triptych *To the Convalescent Woman,* and Kirchner's *Self-Portrait with Cat* of 1920 (the latter two having until 1937 belonged to the Folkwang Museum in Essen). Furthermore, in the same year he bought drawings by Kokoschka, Marc, Kirchner, and Schlemmer. Other works

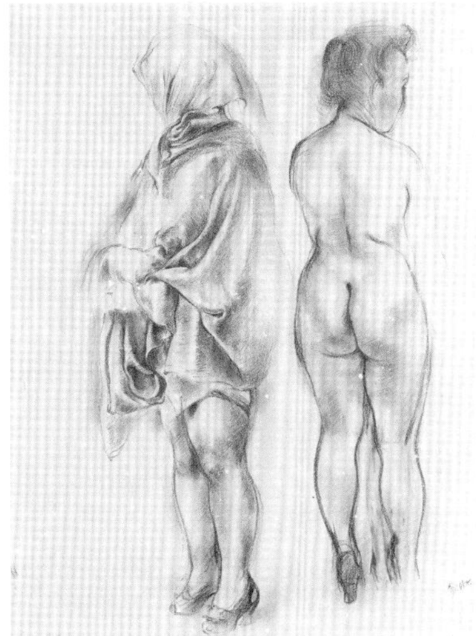

George Grosz (1893–1959), **Two Models and Drapery,** *ca. 1940. Graphite with charcoal, 50 x 39.3 cm. Antonia Paepcke DuBrul Fund, 1989.59.*

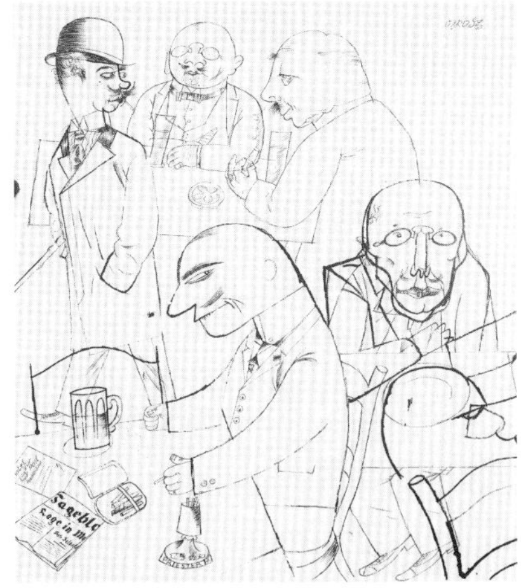

George Grosz (1893–1959), **Cafe,** *ca. 1919. Black ink on gray wove paper, 35.5 x 29.2 cm. Museum purchase, BR34.195.*

coming to the Busch by purchase at this time included paintings by Lissitzky (1949), Mueller (1953), Schmidt-Rottluff (1954), Feininger (1954), Kirchner (1951), and Kokoschka (1952). Major prints and sculpture were also acquired during these years, and the Bauhaus collection grew rapidly, as described below.

This spectacular transformation of the collections naturally attracted enthusiastic donors and supporters. Not least among them was Charles Kuhn himself, whose name is to be found surprisingly often behind the innocuous designation "Anonymous gift" on many exceptionally fine works of art acquired throughout his tenure. The Pittsburgh collector G. David Thompson, who had amassed one of the great collections of modern art, gave works of art (notably the Busch's two paintings by Schlemmer in 1955 and 1956) and money for acquisitions (especially for the magnificent Nolde oil, the *Mulatto,* bought in 1953). In the mid-1950s the Feiningers gave significant works by their contemporaries, including Schmidt-Rottluff, Heckel, Rohlfs, Itten, Schlemmer, and Marcks. Gifts of expressionist, 1920s, and some postwar art also came from nationally renowned collectors such as John Newberry, Erich Cohn, Lessing Rosenwald, Professor and Mrs. John McAndrew, and from dealers such as Rose Fried, Curt Valentin, and J.B. Neumann.

A local collector, Louis W. Black, Harvard AB '26, AM '27, LLB '30, made major contributions to the print collection (adding special strength to the Barlach and Pechstein holdings), and, at his untimely death in 1958, gifts and purchases of prints and drawings in his honor brought in works by Klimt,

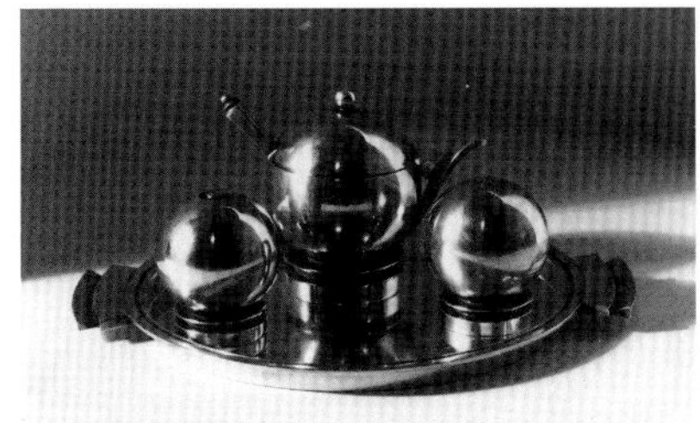

Georg Jensen (1866–1935), **Condiment Set,** *ca. 1930. Silver, tray diam. 17.1 cm. Anonymous gift, BR31.22a–d.*

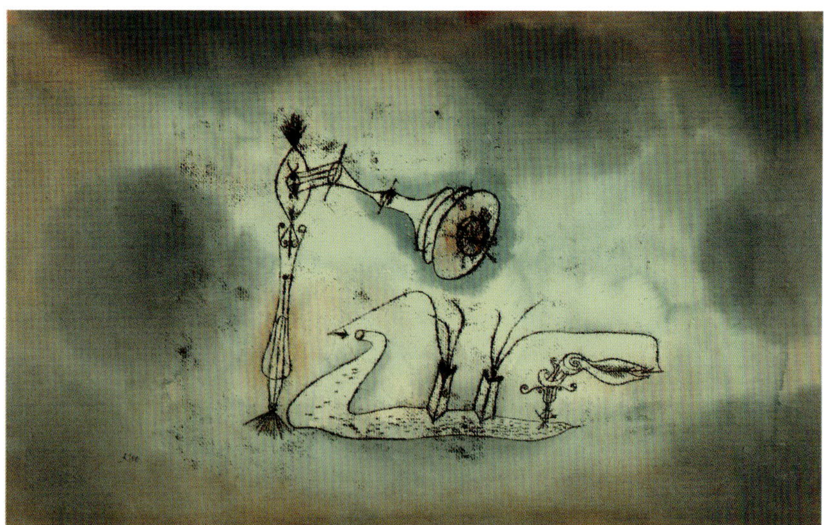

Paul Klee (1879–1940), Apparatus for the Magnetic Treatment of Plants, *1921. Oil transfer drawing and watercolor, 31.1 x 47.9 cm. Museum purchase, BR34.80.*

Macke, Heckel, Kirchner, Klee, Kokoschka, Kubin, Lissitzky, Mueller, and others. The Busch-Reisinger's intense activity in this field in the 1950s was nicely matched by some important acquisitions made by the Fogg Art Museum, notably the arrival in 1955 of three major works by Beckmann: the 1941–42 triptych *The Actors* (a gift of Mrs. Lois Orswell, who also gave a Kolbe sculpture to the Busch-Reisinger in the same year), the 1927 *Portrait of Zeretelli,* and the 1947 *Souvenir of Chicago* (both from Mr. Joseph Pulitzer, Jr., Harvard '36, and his wife). Important works by Klee and Kokoschka also arrived at the Fogg in 1955.

In 1957–58 (by gift) and in 1961 (by bequest), Alexander Dorner, a pioneering museum director in Germany in the 1920s and friend to many avant-garde artists, added to the holdings of abstract constructivist art with major works by Malevich, Gabo, Moholy-Nagy, Lissitzky, and others.

It was also in these key years that the small but useful collection of late nineteenth- and turn-of-the-century works was consolidated through F.F. Beer's gift of works by Trübner, Liebermann, Slevogt, and others. 1953 saw the gift of Corinth's 1899 *Salome,* a work which had been offered to the Museum of Modern Art but refused and guided to the Busch by Kuhn's fellow Harvard graduate, Alfred Barr. Corinth's son also donated a number of drawings by his father to the museum, thereby supplementing other works in the Busch and Fogg. The museum also acquired a late nineteenth-century painting by von Marées (1960), an important figure in the origins of modern German art virtually unrepresented in American collections. The foundation was also laid for a group of Vienna Secession works, described separately below.

By the early 1960s, then, Kuhn's project of building a small but highly select teaching collection of modern art from Central and Northern Europe had largely been accomplished. The growth in this aspect of the collections prompted the 1957 publication of an illustrated checklist of the holdings of German expressionism and abstract art in Harvard collections (sensibly including works in the

Fogg and in the Houghton Library), followed by a supplementary volume in 1967.

Certainly, the intervening three decades have seen many additions to the collections in these areas. The Busch-Reisinger has focused on strengthening the turn-of-the-century collection, with purchases of further works by Corinth (1990) and Trübner (1991) supplementing the 1976 gift of a second painting by von Marées. Noteworthy additions to the core collections of expressionism and abstract art have included paintings by Kupka (1962), Feininger (1964), and Kandinsky (1982, from Mrs. Paul E. Geier); sculpture by Barlach (1967, 1972, 1975, 1991), Beckmann (1976), Kolbe (1965), Kollwitz (1991), Marcks (1962, 1986, 1991), and Mataré (1964, given by Richard L. Feigen, Harvard MBA '54). The collections of works on paper have also been regularly enriched by pieces by all the important artists represented in Kuhn's accession lists. Significant additions include groups of works by Barlach, Heckel, Kandinsky, Kirchner, Klee, Kollwitz, Lehmbruck, Marcks, and Nolde. In 1974, Mrs. Walter Gropius gave the museum the portfolios of prints by many leading artists of the day published by the Bauhaus from 1921 to 1923. In 1987, the bequest of the social psychiatrist Fredric Wertham brought a major group of constructivist and related works to the Busch-Reisinger (as well as numerous pieces to other Harvard repositories), including a substantial group of works by Lissitzky and pieces by Moholy-Nagy, Dexel, Schwitters, van Doesburg, and others. The acquisition of drawings and prints by Grosz has taken on particular importance, as the museum has tried to build up holdings to match the archive of written and printed Grosz materials established at the Houghton Library by the artist's heirs.

The Fogg has continued to make complementary acquisitions, including paintings by Munch (1963), Klee (1962), Jawlensky (1965), Beckmann (1975), and two by Ernst (1976 and 1979), as well as prints and drawings by German, Swiss, and Austrian artists of the period. As always, the Busch-Reisinger's holdings must be seen in the light of cognate collections at the Fogg and elsewhere at Harvard.

Nevertheless, the generalization broadly holds true that, except in the field of contemporary art (that is, after 1945), the new acquisitions have largely dotted the i's and crossed the t's of Kuhn's decisive acquisition campaign of the 1950s.

This has inevitably led to the welcome circumstance that the Busch-Reisinger's collection of modern art bears quite a personal stamp. In a way, it reflects a particular interpretation of German and related art of the period, an interpretation that is perhaps already inherent in Kuhn's two key purchases in his first decade as

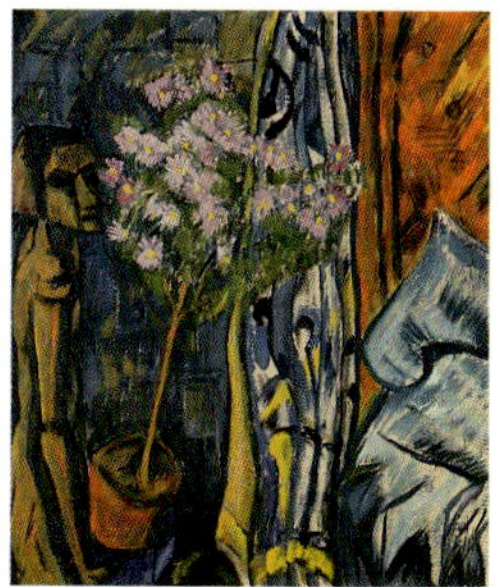
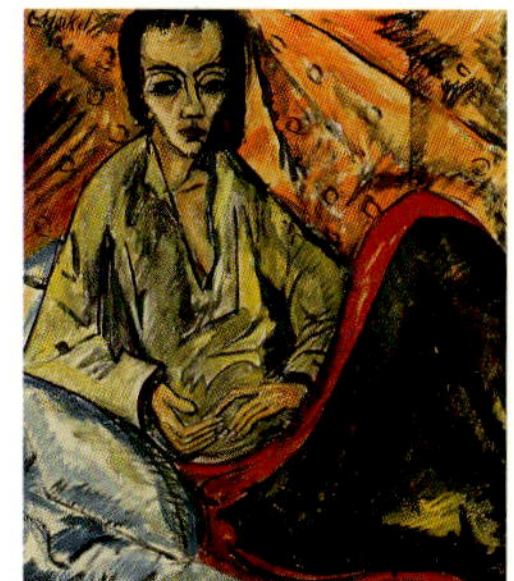
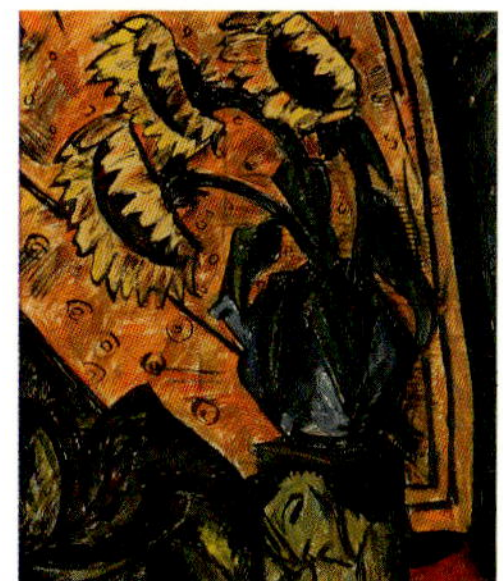

Erich Heckel (1883–1970), To the Convalescent Woman, 1912–13. Oil, each panel 81.3 x 70.8 cm. Edmée Busch Greenough Fund, BR50.415a–c.

curator, the Barlach *Crippled Beggar* and the Beckmann *Self-Portrait*. Both in their own way speak of the redemptive, utopian side of German art of the period.

The *Self-Portrait* is perhaps Beckmann's most confident, assertive picture, showing the artist in full control, powerful and self-assured. Kuhn did not buy examples of the more anguished, pessimistic Beckmann of the early 1920s (or of the again more troubled period of the 1930s and 1940s). The Barlach shows the crippled beggar as a member of the Community of Saints (the program for the projected sixteen figures on the church facade), raising his face in religious striving with the promise of release. A similar theme of overcoming tribulation emerges in the Heckel triptych, which shows not a sick woman, but a convalescent under the healing influence of the plants and sculpture in the side panels, just as Kirchner's self-portrait also shows him recovering from a nervous breakdown in the regenerative atmosphere of the Swiss Alps, attended by flowers and a cat. Pictures of nudes in an

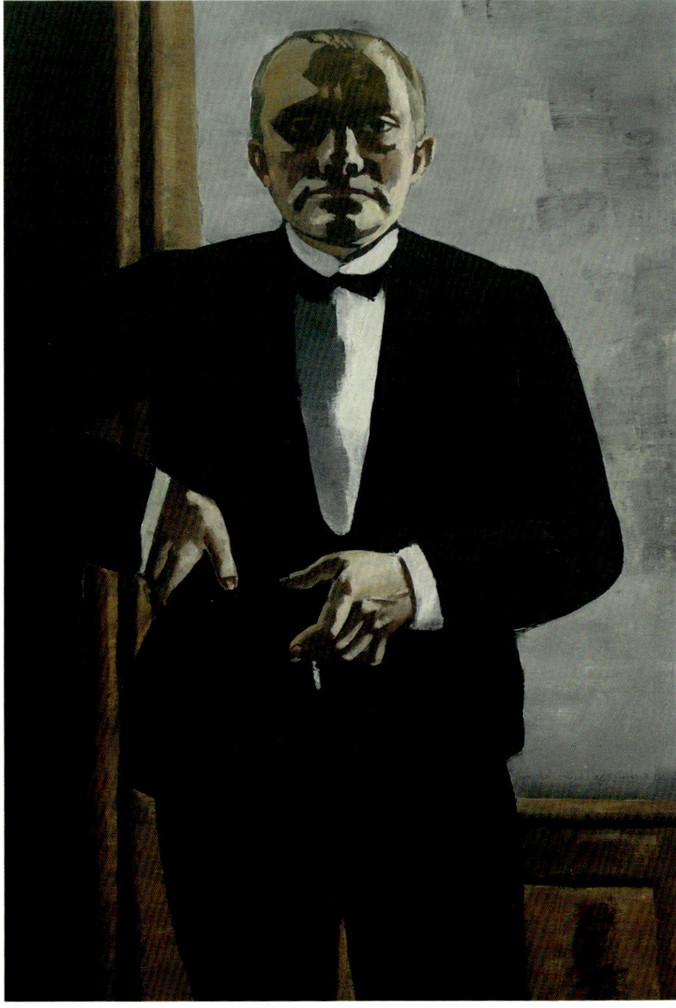

Max Beckmann (1884–1950), Self-Portrait in Tuxedo, 1927. Oil, 139.5 x 95.5 cm. Museum purchase, BR41.37.

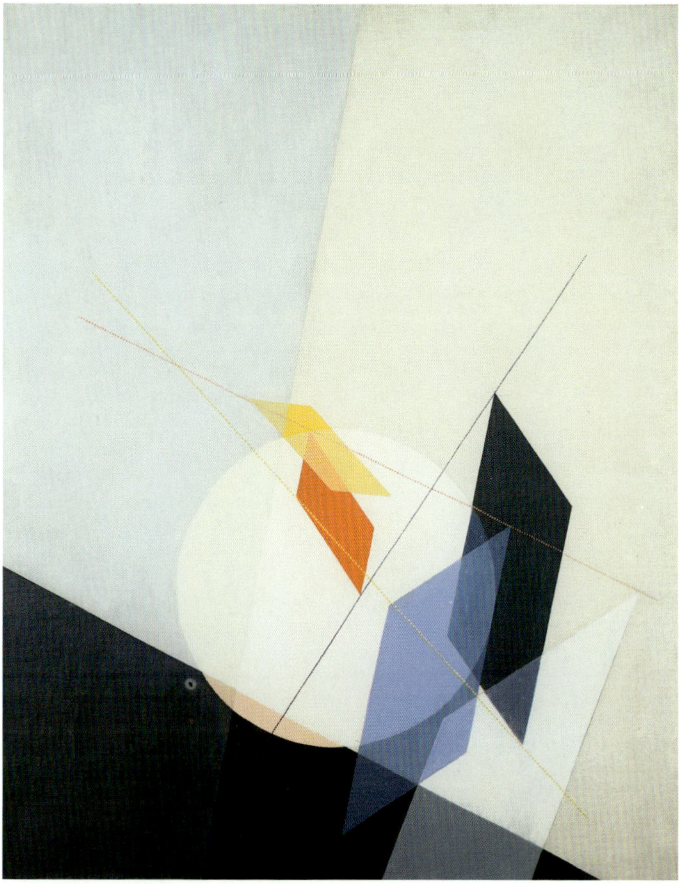

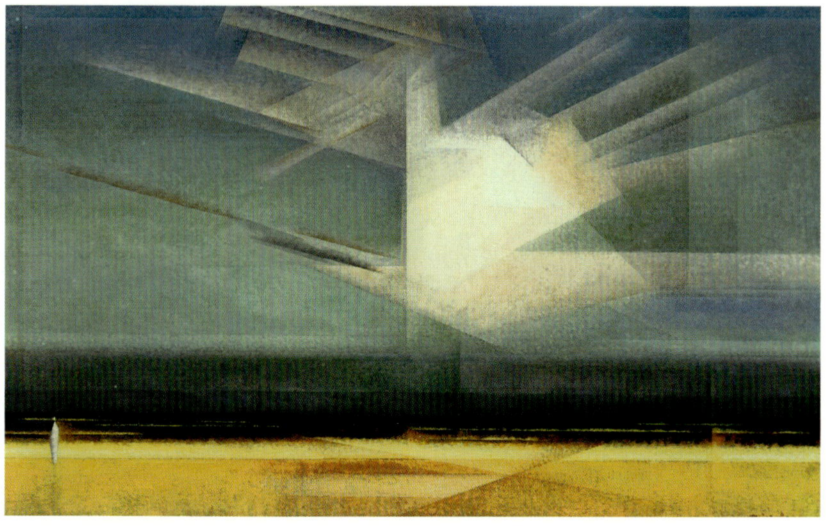

Laszlo Moholy-Nagy (1895–1946), A 18, 1927. Oil, 95.9 x 75.2 cm. Museum purchase, BR50.416.

Lyonel Feininger (1871–1956), Bird Cloud, 1926. Oil, 43.8 x 71.1 cm. Purchase in memory of Eda K. Loeb, BR50.414.

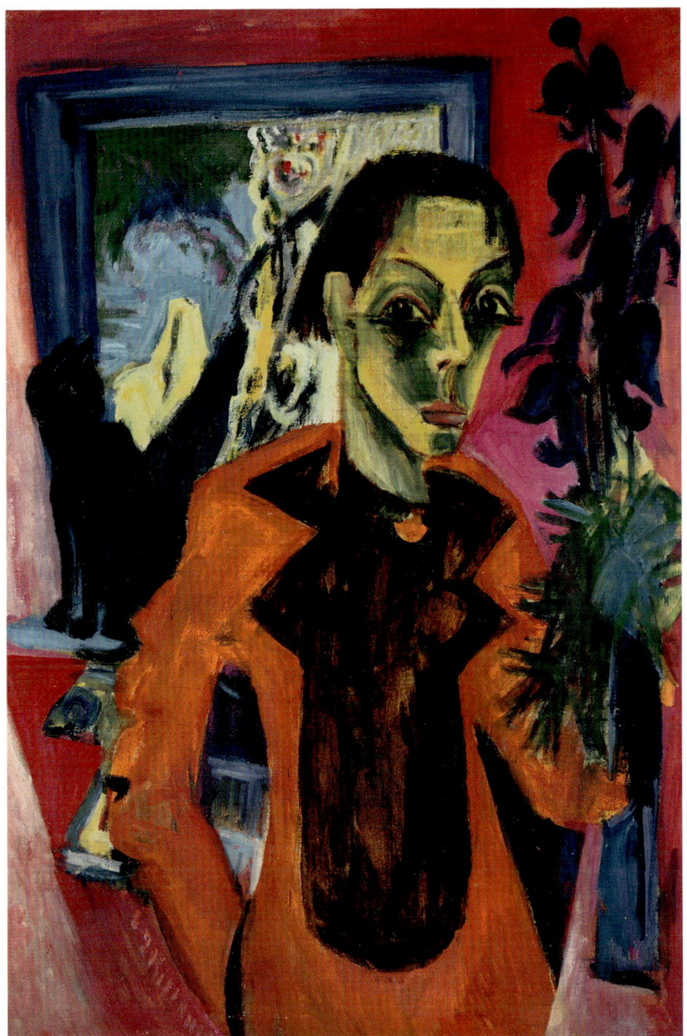

Ernst Ludwig Kirchner (1880–1938), Self-Portrait with Cat, 1920. Oil, 120.6 x 80 cm. Museum purchase, BR50.12.

idyllic landscape (Schmidt-Rottluff, Heckel, etc.), of the radiant power of so-called primitive peoples (Nolde), or of the harmony of humans, buildings, and nature (Feininger) could be adduced to underline the tendency. There is also the negative evidence that very little of the virulently sociocritical art of Grosz and Dix or the apparently nihilistic antics of Dada artists entered the collection through Kuhn.

The Bauhaus collection (see separate description) and the related holdings of constructivism also speak of the passionately optimistic view that art could and should contribute models and ideals for the restructuring of society. In general, these still underexplored collections offer a useful antidote both to any convenient polarization between expressionism and the geometric abstraction of the years between the wars, and to the clichéd understanding of Germanic art as one of torture and torment expressed through an agitated soul. In its very international-

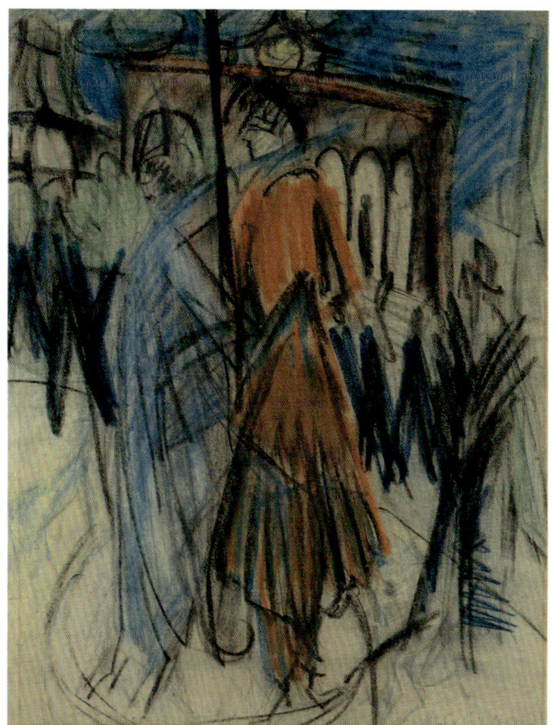

Ernst Ludwig Kirchner (1880–1938), Berlin Street Scene (Potsdamer Platz), 1913. Colored chalk, 68.4 x 48.3 cm. Association Fund, BR50.616.

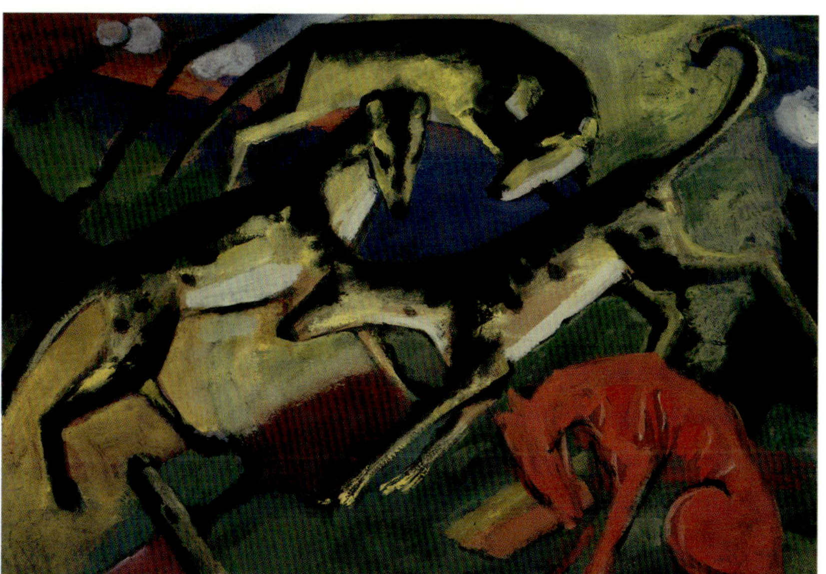

Franz Marc (1880–1916), **Playing Dogs,** *ca. 1912. Gouache, 38.1 x 54.6 cm. Museum purchase, BR50.451.*

ism (encompassing Austrian, Swiss, German, Hungarian, Dutch, and Russian artists, to mention only some of the nationalities), the Busch collection can also work against any easily narrow definition of so-called German art.

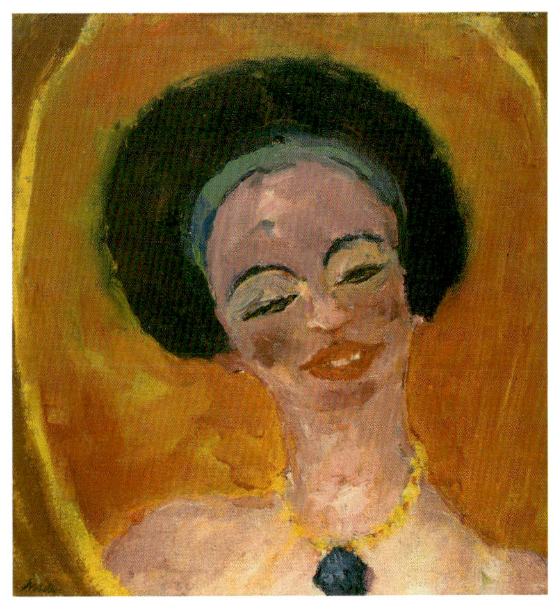

Emil Nolde (1867–1956), Mulatto, *1915. Oil, 77.5 x 73 cm. Museum purchase, BR54.117.*

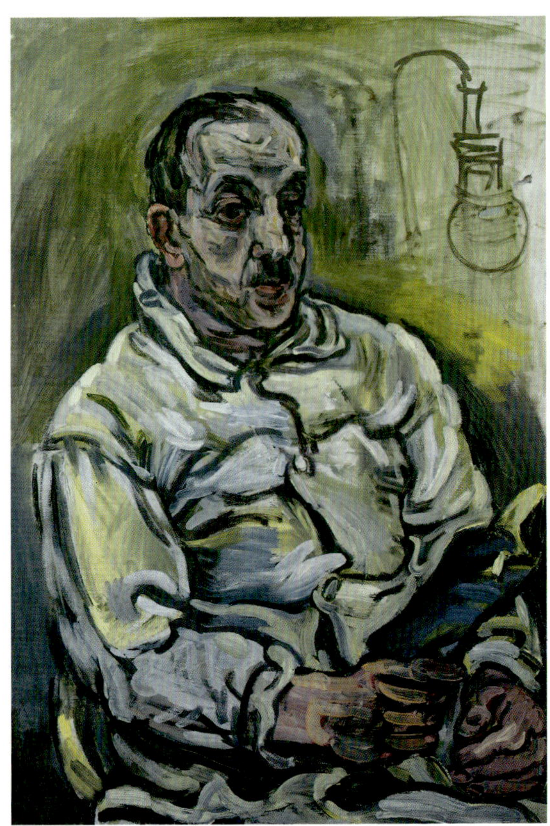

Oskar Kokoschka (1886–1980), Portrait of Dr. Heinrich von Neumann, *1916. Oil, 90.1 x 59.9 cm. Association Fund, BR52.21.*

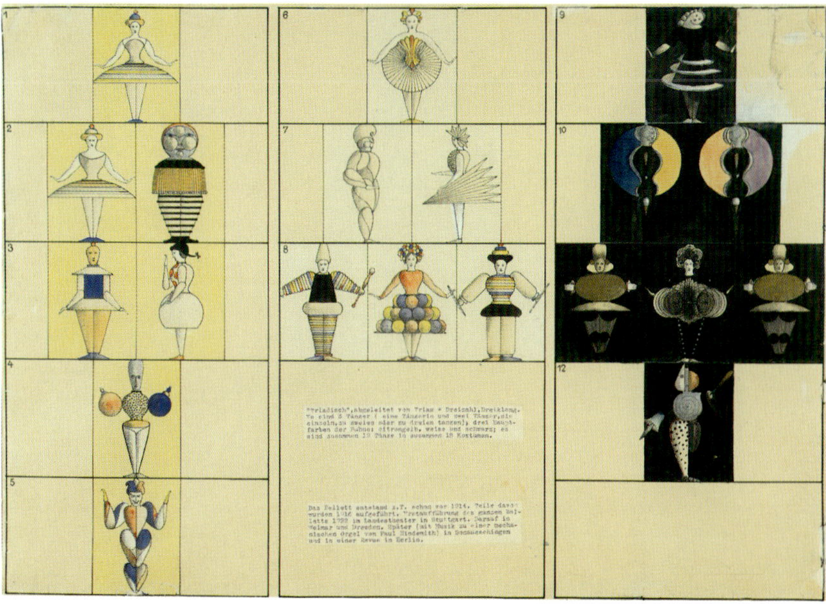

Oskar Schlemmer (1888–1943), **Costume Designs for the "Triadic Ballet,"** *ca. 1922. Ink, gouache, metallic powder, graphite, and collage, 38.1 x 53.3 cm. Museum purchase, BR50.428.*

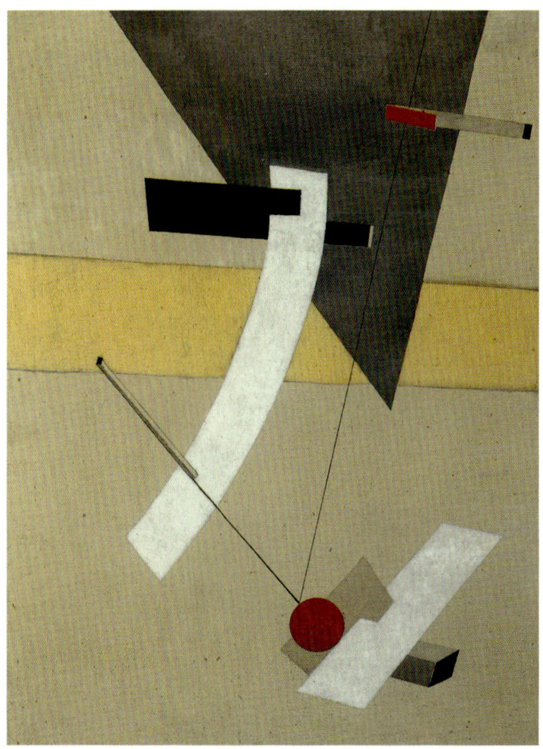

El Lissitzky (1890–1941), **Proun 12 E,** *1923. Oil, 57.1 x 42.5 cm. Association Fund, BR49.303.*

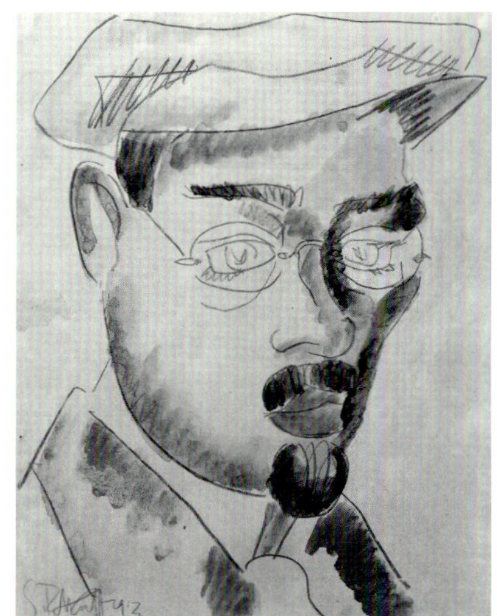

Karl Schmidt-Rottluff (1884–1976), Self-Portrait, 1913. Watercolor and black crayon on brown paper, 43.2 x 33 cm. Gift of Mr. and Mrs. Lyonel Feininger, BR54.119.

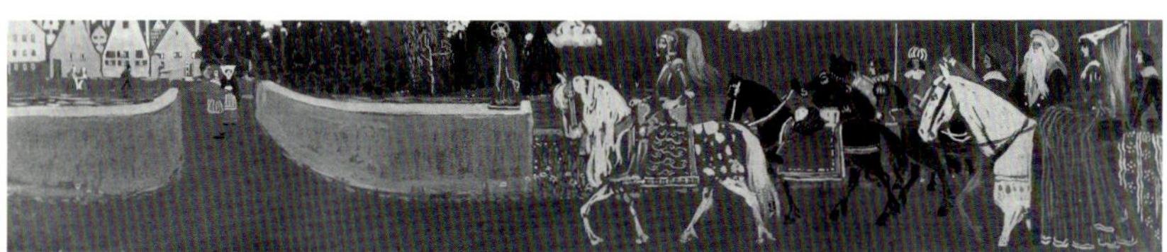

Wassily Kandinsky (1866–1944), Festival, ca. 1903. Gouache on cardboard, 20 x 90 cm. Purchase with funds realized from a gift of Curt Valentin, BR58.1.

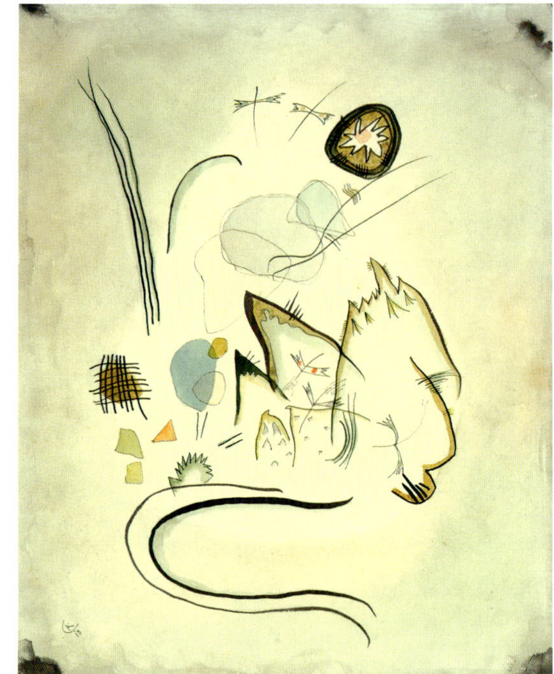

Wassily Kandinsky (1866–1944), Untitled, 1918. Watercolor and black ink over graphite on cream paper, 29 x 23 cm. Anonymous gift in memory of Curt Valentin, BR56.50.

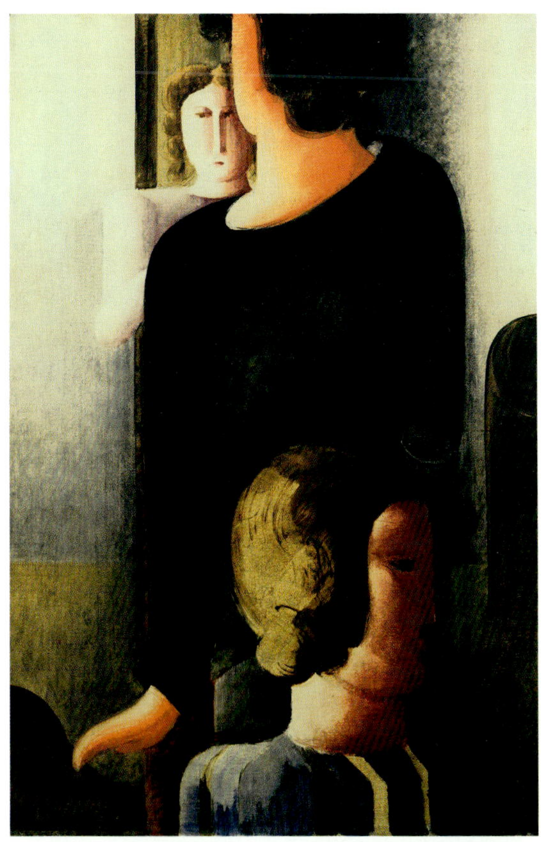

Oskar Schlemmer (1888–1943), Three Figures with Furniture-Like Forms, *1929. Oil, 90.9 x 60.3 cm. Gift of G. David Thompson, BR55.447.*

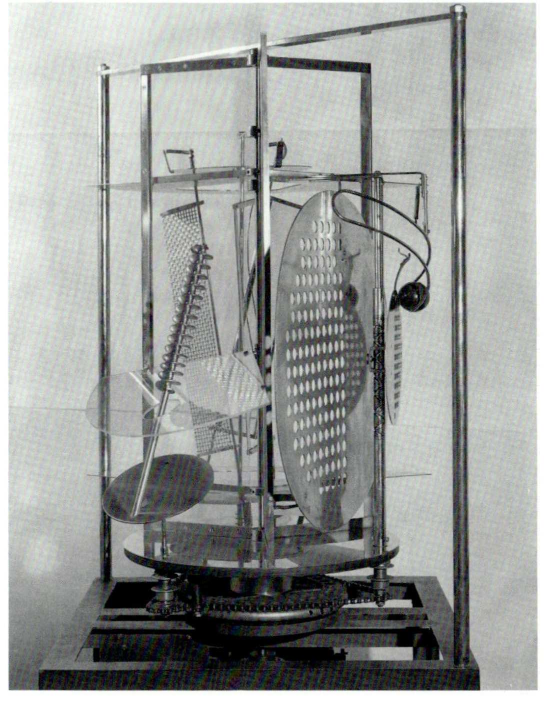

Laszlo Moholy-Nagy (1895–1946), Light-Space Modulator, *1923–30. Kinetic sculpture of steel, plastic, wood, and other materials with electric motor, h. 151.1 cm. Gift of Sibyl Moholy-Nagy, BR56.5.*

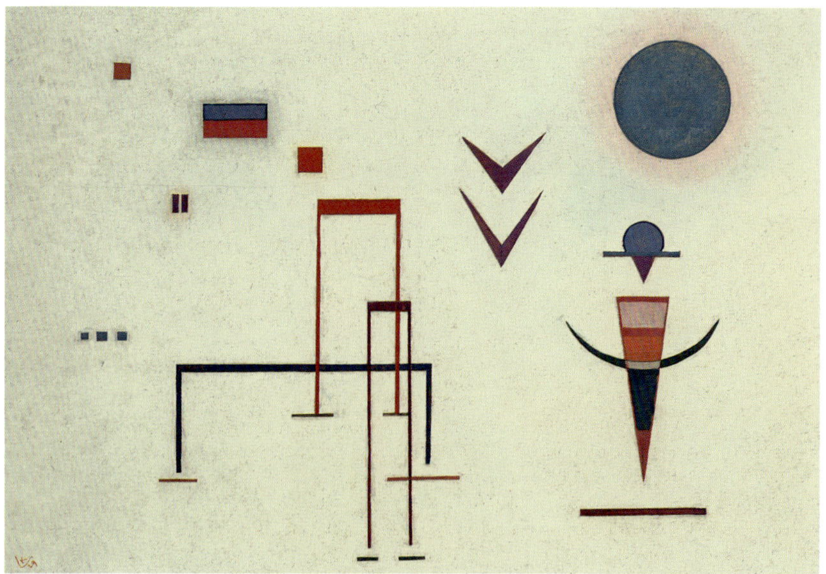

Wassily Kandinsky (1866–1944), Jocular Sounds, 1929. Oil on cardboard, 34.9 x 48.9 cm. Association Fund and in memory of Eda K. Loeb, BR56.54.

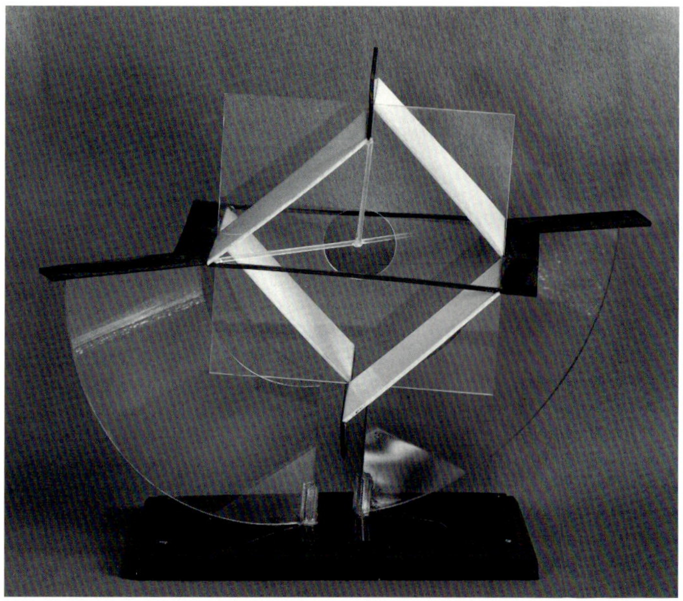

Naum Gabo (1890–1977), Construction in Space with Balance on Two Points, 1925. Black, white, and transparent plastics, h. 25.6 cm. Gift of Lydia Dorner in memory of Dr. Alexander Dorner, BR58.46.

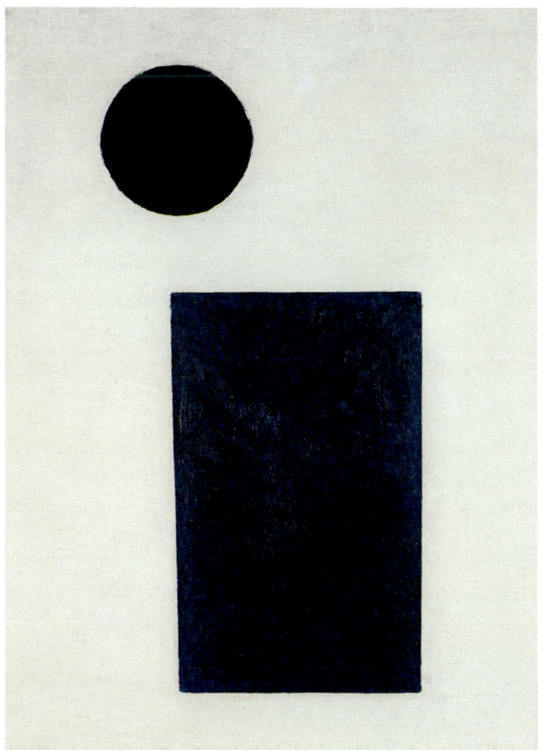

Kasimir Malevich (1878–1935), Suprematist Painting, Rectangle and Circle, 1915. Oil, 43.1 x 30.7 cm. Alexander Dorner Trust, BR57.128.

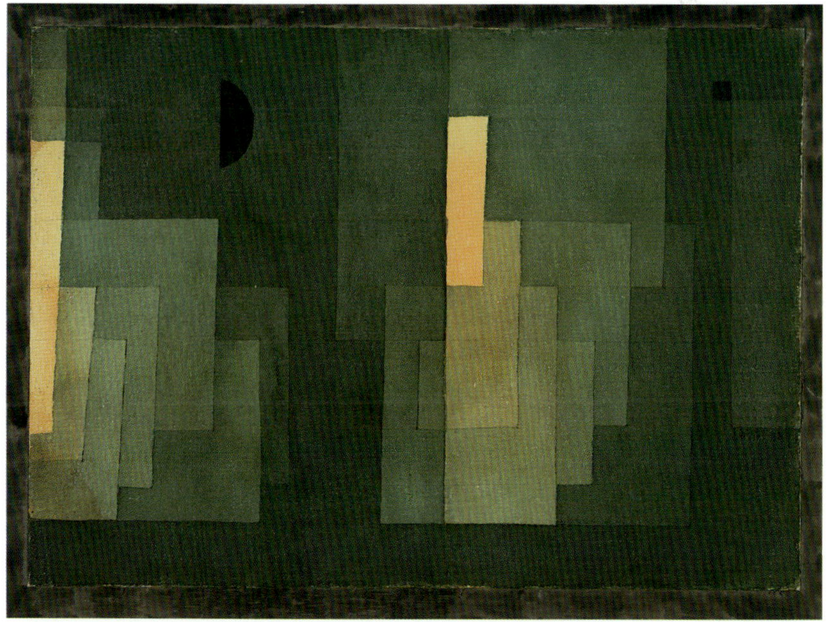

Paul Klee (1879–1940), **Green-Orange Gradation with Black Half Moon,** *1922. Black ink and watercolor over graphite, 29.9 x 39.4 cm. Association Fund, BR62.86.*

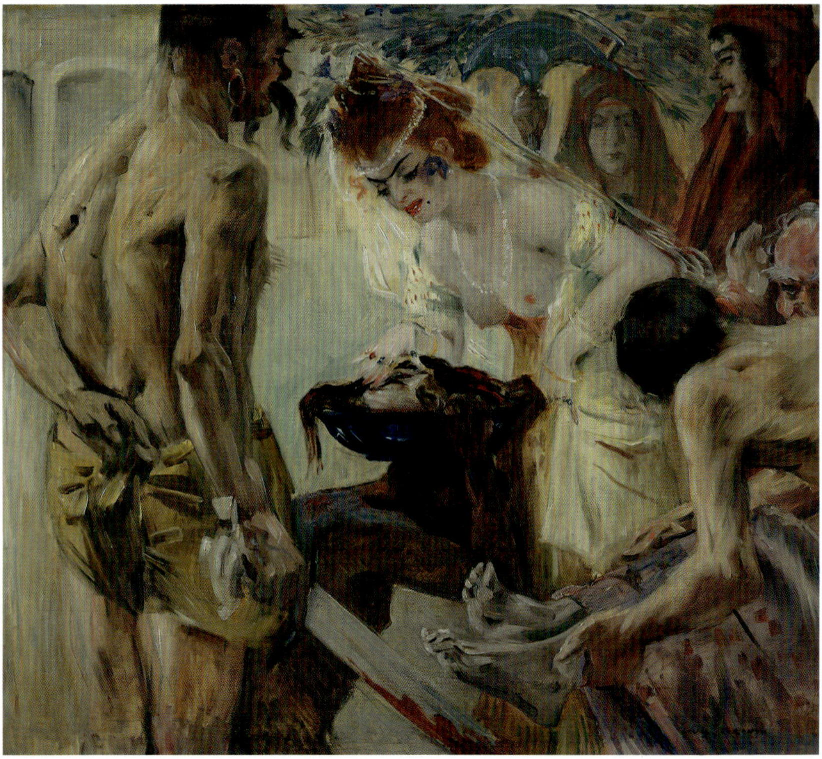

Lovis Corinth (1858–1925), Salome, 1899. Oil, 76.2 x 83.3 cm. Gift of Hans H.A. Meyn, BR53.60.

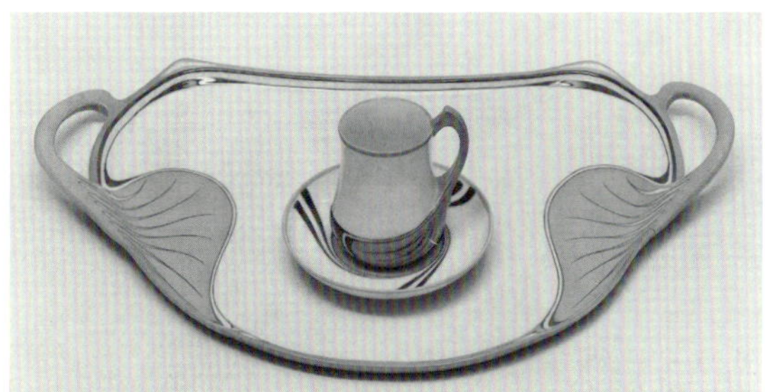

Otto Edouard Gottfried Voigt (1870–1949), modeler, Meissen manufacture, Cup, Saucer, and Tray, 1904. Porcelain, cup h. 8.3 cm., saucer diam. 13.3 cm., tray 47.6 x 31 cm. Gift of Mr. J. Jonathan Joseph, BR70.10 a–c.

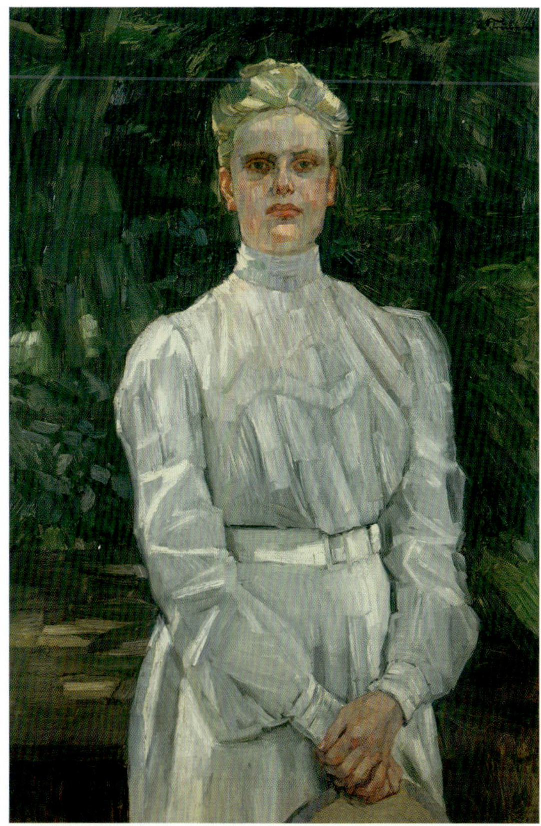

Wilhelm Trübner (1851–1917), Fraülein Maria Wüsthoff, 1901. Oil, 110.5 x 73.5 cm. Richard Norton Memorial Fund and through the generosity of the Rudolf Siedersleben'sche Otto Wolff-Foundation and Melvin R. Seiden, 1990.82.

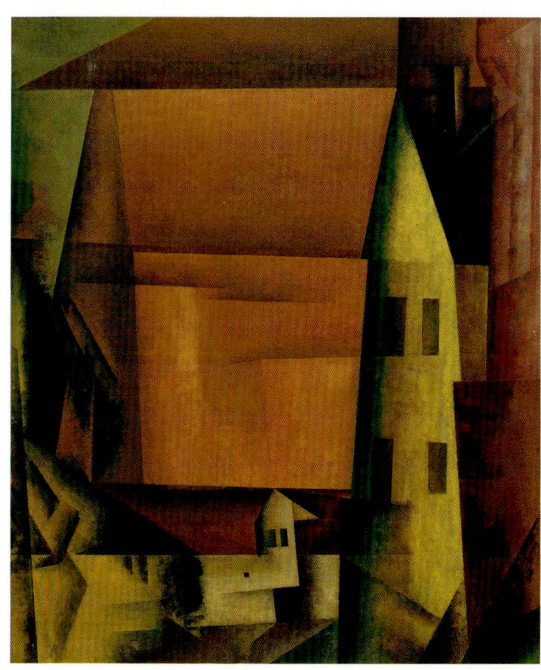

Lyonel Feininger (1871–1956), Gross-Kromsdorf III, 1921. Oil, 100 x 80 cm. Gift of Julia Feininger, BR64.12.

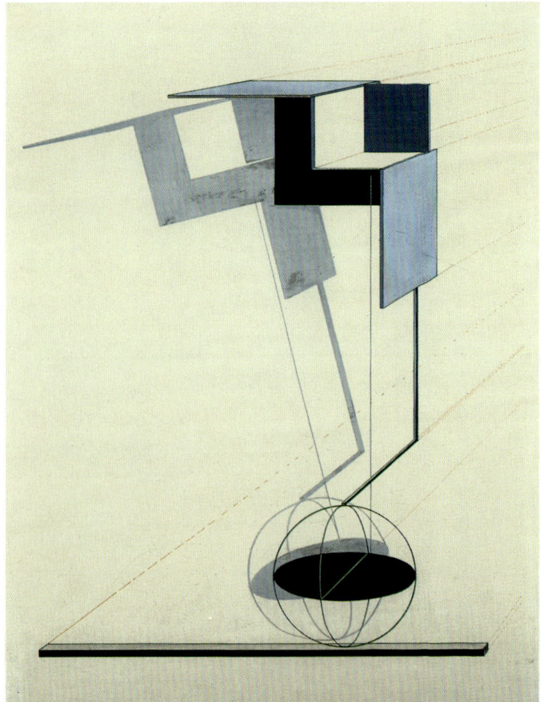

El Lissitzky (1890–1941), Proun (Study for a lithograph in the Kestner Portfolio), 1922–23. Gouache with red and black inks, 59 x 43.4 cm. The Fredric Wertham Collection, Gift of his wife Hesketh, 1987.62.

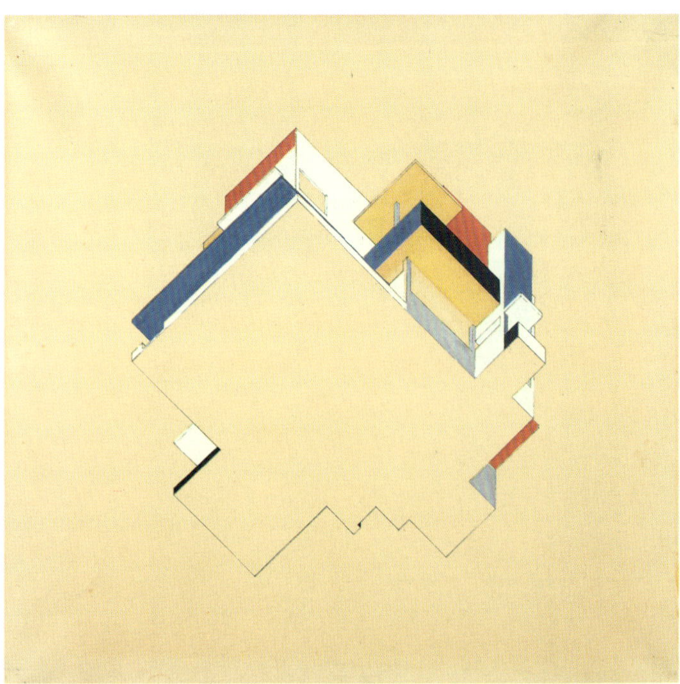

Theo van Doesburg (1883–1931), Construction of Colors, 1923. Gouache and graphite over print, 57 x 57 cm. The Fredric Wertham Collection, Gift of his wife Hesketh, 1987.87.

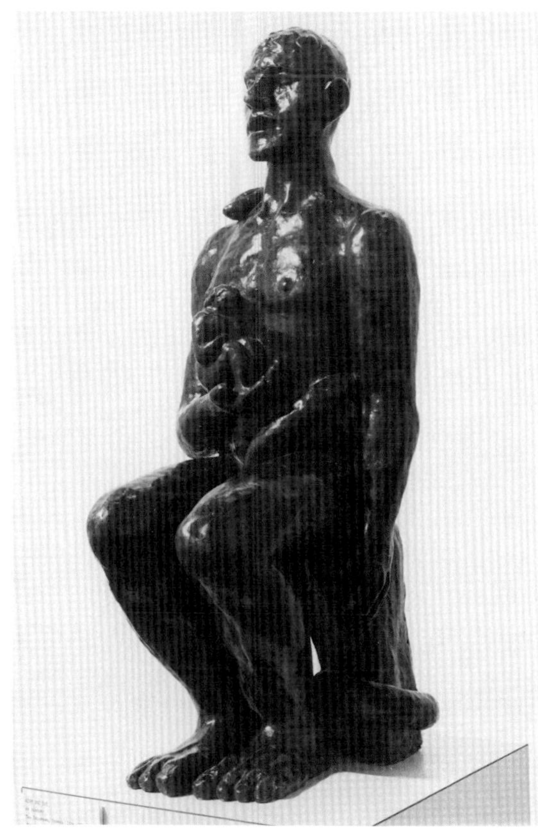

Left: *Max Beckmann (1884–1950),* Adam and Eve, *1936. Bronze, h. 83.3 cm. Gift of Mr. and Mrs. Irving Rabb, BR76.5.*

Below: *Ernst Barlach (1870–1938),* The Avenger, *1914. Bronze, h. 44.5 cm. Gift of Mr. Norbert Schimmel, BR72.57.*

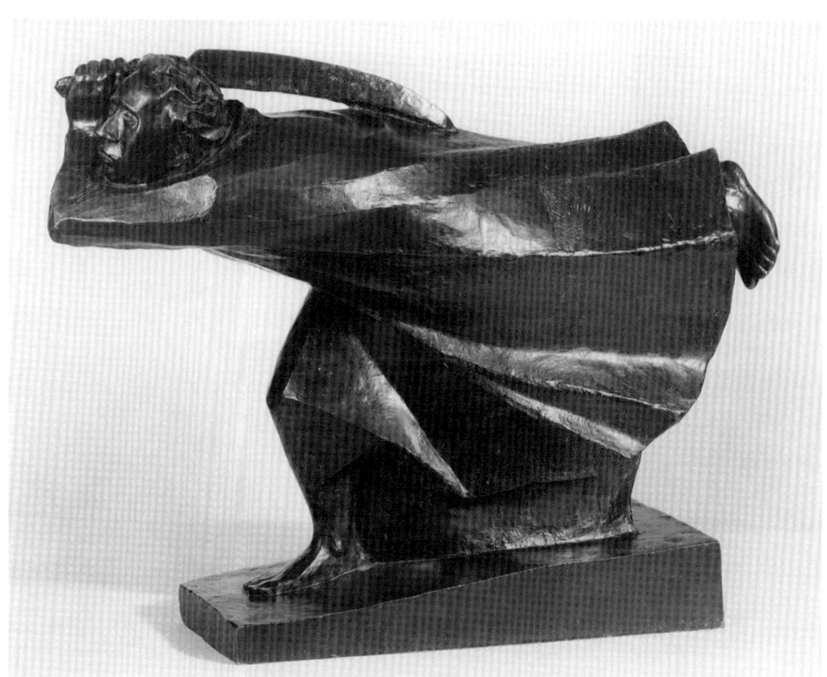

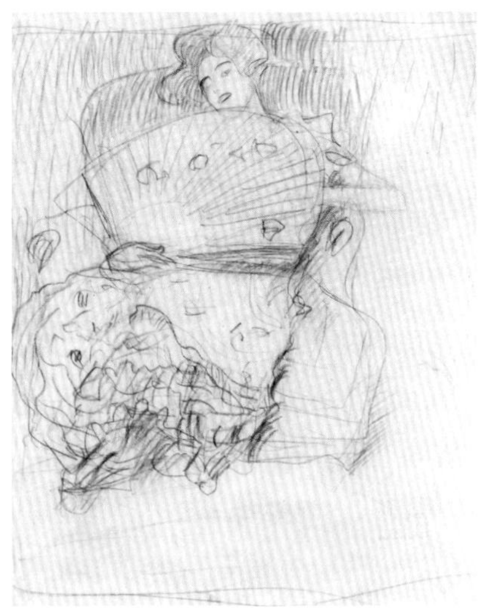

Gustav Klimt (1862–1918), Lady with a Fan, ca. 1908. Charcoal with graphite on brown wove paper, 45.7 x 31.1 cm. Purchase in memory of Louis W. Black, 1959.34.

Vienna Secession

Within the modern collections, works associated with the Vienna Secession form a useful and impressive group. The artistic renaissance in turn-of-the-century Austria encompassed many of the key achievements of modern art and design. The Busch-Reisinger holdings permit a concentrated but illuminating insight into the period.

As with so much else, this part of the collection was essentially formed in the 1950s. Also typically, it began with the applied arts: in 1950, a bar set of glassware designed by Adolf Loos for the Lobmeyr firm was purchased, and in 1955 a substantial set of over forty fabric designs by Czescka, Hoffmann, Moser, Wimmer, and others was given by the Metropolitan Museum of Art. It was also in the 1950s that the museum's one great painting from this era arrived at Harvard, Klimt's *Pear Tree*, to be joined by the end of the decade by drawings by Klimt, Hoffmann, and Schiele (another Schiele drawing was added in 1968). The various paintings, drawings, prints, and illustrations by Kokoschka in the other Harvard collections can also be seen in this context.

A second concerted campaign to acquire Austrian art of the early twentieth century was initiated by curator John David Farmer around 1970. This added a fashion design by Wimmer, a poster design by Löffler, and several pieces of decorative arts, including an example of Hoffmann's chair for the Purkersdorf Sanatorium. In addition to

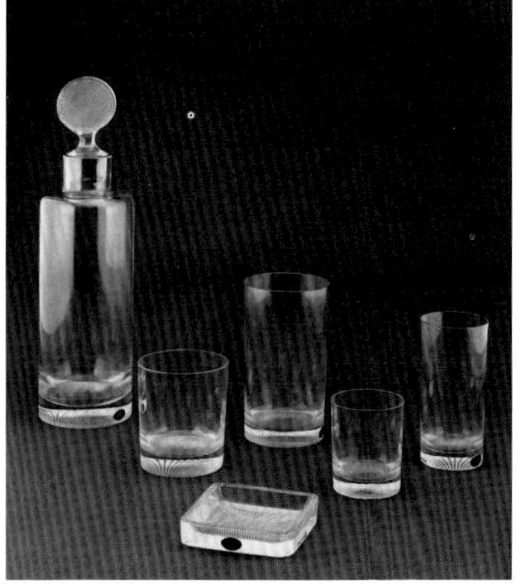

Adolf Loos (1870–1933), Lobmeyr manufacture, Bar Set, 1931. Engraved glass, decanter h. 29.8 cm. Museum purchase, BR50.438–43.

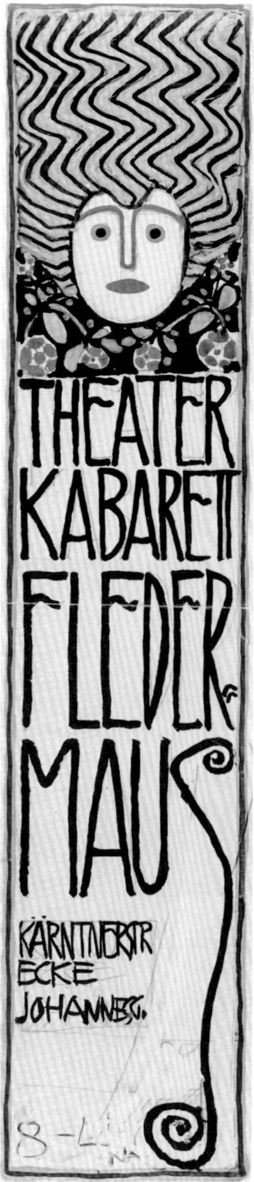

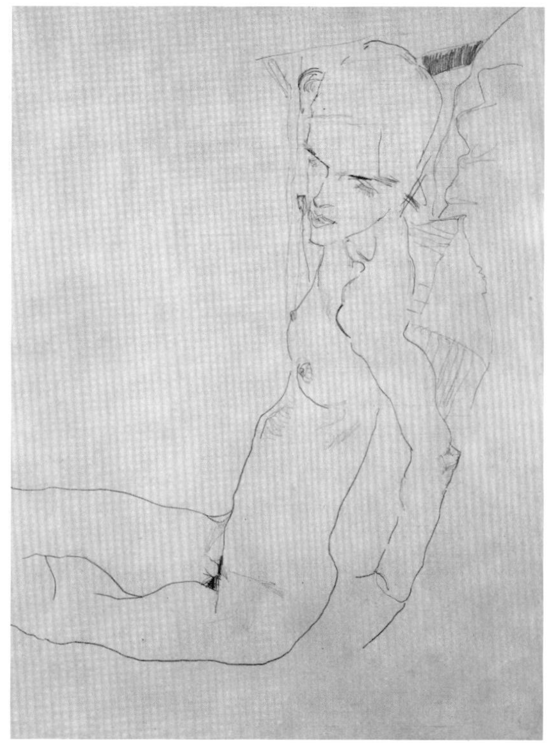

Egon Schiele (1890–1918), Seated Nude, *1911. Graphite, 53.6 x 38.1 cm. Anonymous gift, BR56.7.*

Bertold Löffler (1874–1960), Study for poster: Theater Kabarett Fledermaus, *ca. 1907–8. Ink and gouache over graphite, 58.1 x 22.2 cm. Purchase in memory of Eda K. Loeb, BR70.18.*

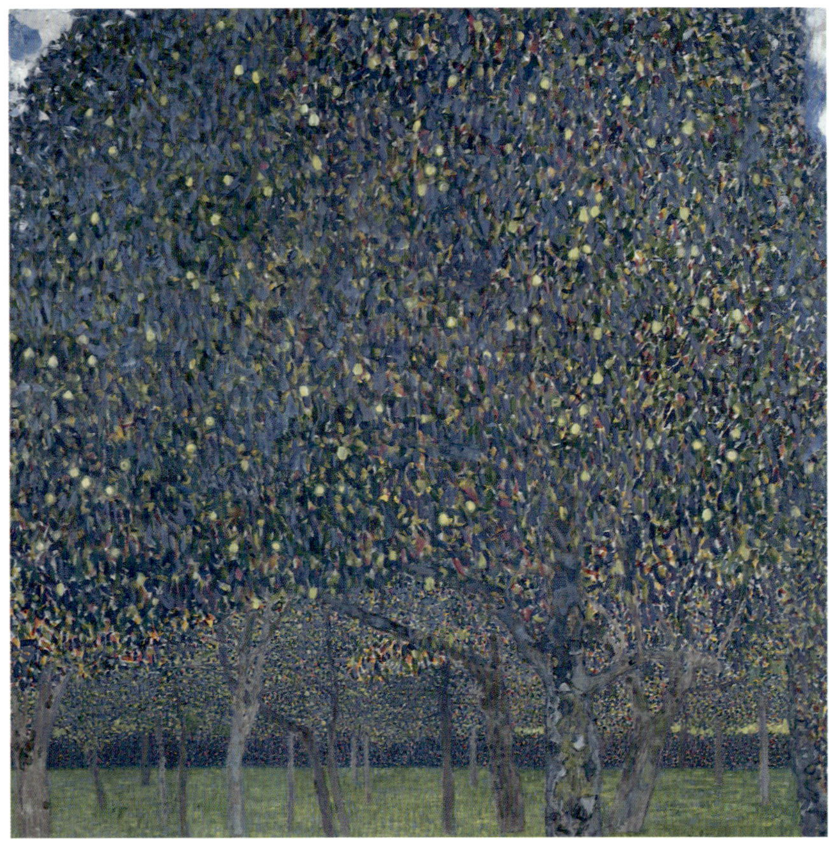

Gustav Klimt (1862–1918), Pear Tree, *1903. Oil and casein, 101 x 101 cm. Gift of Otto Kallir, BR66.4.*

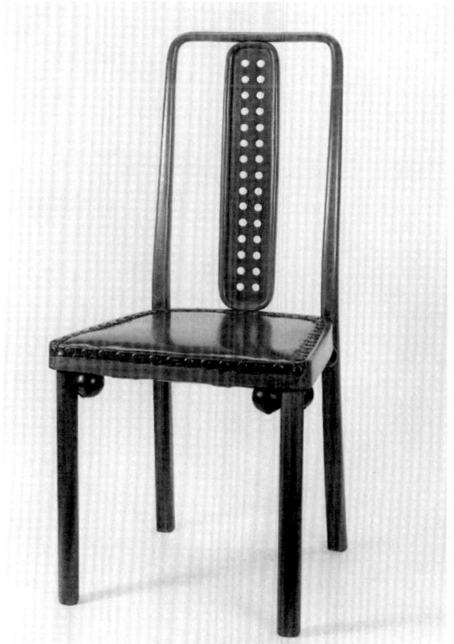

Josef Hoffmann (1870–1956). Chair for the Purkersdorf Sanatorium, ca. 1903–6. Wood, nails, and leather, h. 99.0 cm. Museum purchase, BR71.226.

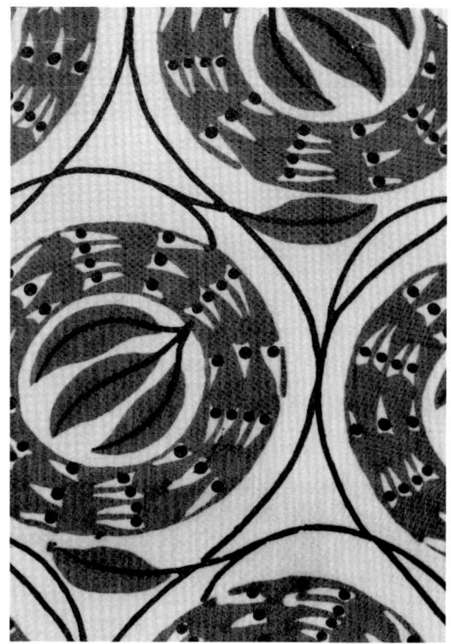

Josef Hoffmann (1870–1956). Printed textile sample, ca. 1906–8. Silk, 14.5 x 10.2 cm. Gift of the Metropolitan Museum of Art, BR55.48.

the Busch holdings, the Fogg offers major drawings by Schiele, Hoffmann, and Klimt, while the University's Houghton Library has many fine examples of typographical and book design of this period.

The Bauhaus Collections

At the end of World War II, the future direction of the museum was very uncertain. Most of its original works of art were stored at the Fogg and there were no plans to move them back; the library and slide collections were being distributed between the Fogg and Widener Library; and part of the gallery space was being used for the storage and distribution of war surplus material.

Acknowledging these changed circumstances, Kuhn decided to focus on research. In 1946 he envisioned a center "for the study of Germanic culture" based on the museum's extensive collection of reproductions, which were still housed in Adolphus Busch Hall. This proposal persisted when a substantial influx of new money in the late 1940s enabled the museum to regain its vitality. Given Kuhn's long-standing interest in design and in contemporary art (and the museum's tradition of not distinguishing too firmly between high and applied arts), it was logical that a research collection would have as a major focus the Bauhaus, Germany's influential art-and-design school whose dates coincided with those of the Weimar Republic, 1919 to 1933. In 1971 Kuhn wrote that at the end of World War II, "defeated Germany had neither the resources nor the will to undertake such a task, although the value of such a collection to art historians, educators, industrial designers, architects, and city planners was clear."

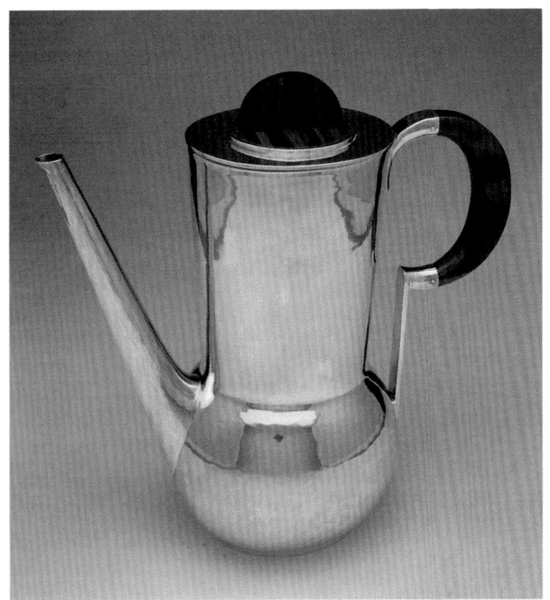

Christian Dell (1893–1974) Coffee Pot, 1925. Silver with zebra wood handles, h. 24.8 cm. Anonymous gift, BR53.85.

Many Bauhaus materials were already in the United States and had been exhibited before World War II. Before the outbreak of war in 1939, several Bauhaus masters and students had emigrated to America; a number had collaborated on the famous 1938 exhibition on the Bauhaus at the Museum of Modern Art. Walter Gropius, founder of the Bauhaus, had been at Harvard as professor of architecture and chairman of the Department of Architecture since 1937. In 1947, Kuhn enlisted Gropius's assistance in locating former Bauhaus associates.

From 1948 on, items of every description flowed in. Donations came from former Bauhaus faculty members Josef and Anni Albers, Mies van der Rohe, Herbert Bayer, Lyonel Feininger, Hannes Meyer, Ludwig Hilberseimer, and Gunta Stadler-Stölzl. Gifts also came from former Bauhaus students Howard Dearstyne, Ludwig Hirschfeld-Mack, and Hannes Beckmann. Sibyl Moholy-Nagy donated works by her late husband Laszlo. Lydia Dorner gave works of art and personal

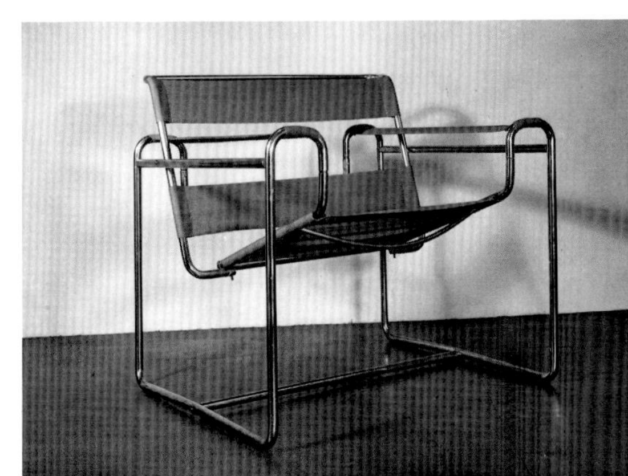

Marcel Breuer (1902–81), Tubular Steel Chair, 1927– 28. Nickel-plated steel tubing with canvas, h. 75.5 cm. Anonymous gift, BR48.27.

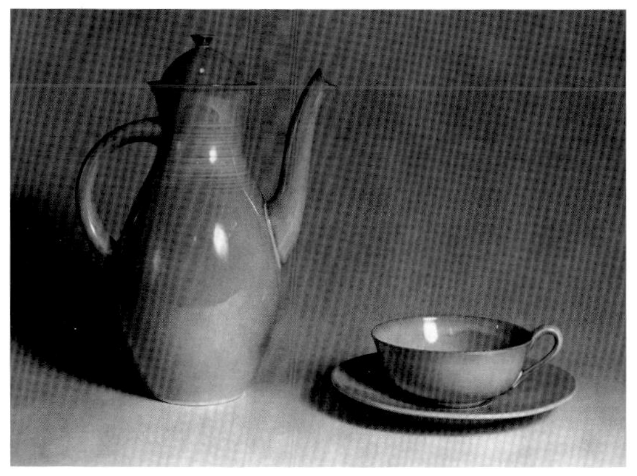

Otto Lindig (1895–1966),
Coffee Pot, Cup and Saucer,
1923–24. Glazed pottery,
pot h. 25cm.; saucer diam.
17.2 cm.; cup diam. 11.4
cm. Anonymous gift,
BR31.89,90.

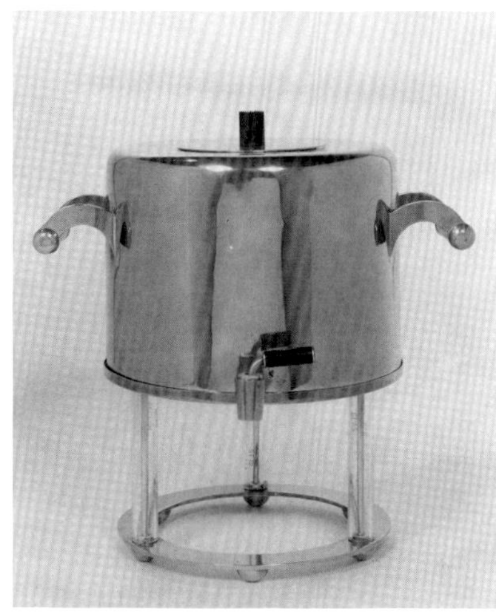

Marianne Brandt (1893–1983), *Tea Urn,*
1925. Silverplate with ebony handles and
glass legs, h. 27 cm. Gift of Walter Gropius,
BR49.260.

papers from her late husband Alexander, former director of the Landesmuseum in Hanover and a major promoter of abstract art. Julia Feininger donated five thousand of her late husband's drawings along with unfinished oil paintings and documentary materials (see separate description of this archive). Gropius himself provided the museum with glass, wood and metalwork, furniture, textiles, and documentary photographs, as well as his personal correspondence and architectural archive (see separate description of the Gropius holdings).

Included in the Bauhaus study collections are class notes, student exercises, pamphlets, photographs, wallpaper, furniture, metal and woodwork, textiles, and typography. For a brief period there were plans to devote a section of the collections to the influence of Bauhaus instruction concepts on American art and architectural institutions, but it soon became apparent that the Bauhaus influence was so prevalent that it would be out of the question to document it completely.

The "Bauhaus Collections" is a loose definition comprising works done not only at the Bauhaus, but by *Bauhäusler* before and after the dates of the school itself, as well as works by students taught on the Bauhaus model. The Busch-Reisinger also contains works in a similar spirit by those who had a strong influence on the school though not officially connected with it, like the constructivists Theo van Doesburg, Walter Dexel, and El Lissitzky, especially from the years 1921 to 1924. The collection ranges from major oil paintings to documentary photographs of textiles; a number of the paintings, drawings, sculpture, and prints are described in other sections of this volume.

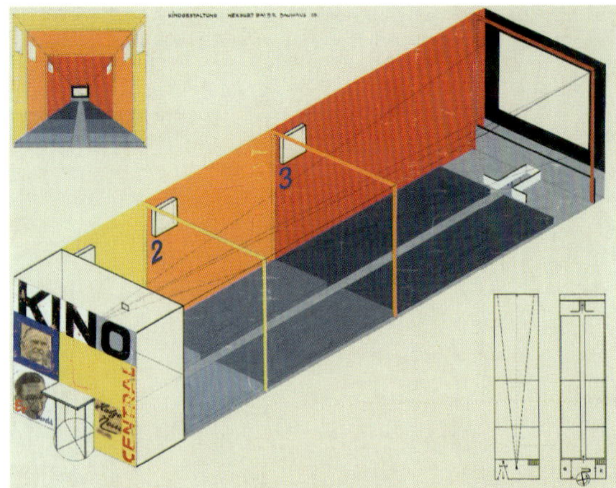

Herbert Bayer (1900–1985),
Design for Cinema, *1925.*
Gouache, ink, graphite, and
collage, 45.7 x 59.7 cm. Gift
of the Artist, BR48.97.

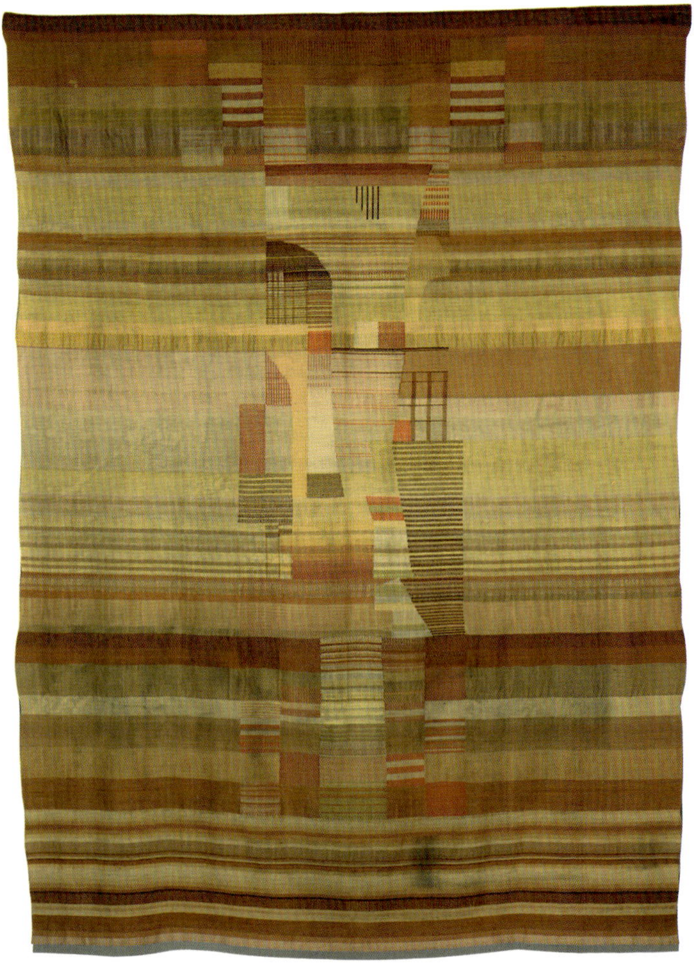

**Gunta Stadler-Stölzl (1897–1983), Tapestry, *1922–23. Cotton, wool, and
linen, 256 x 188 cm. Association Fund, BR49.669.***

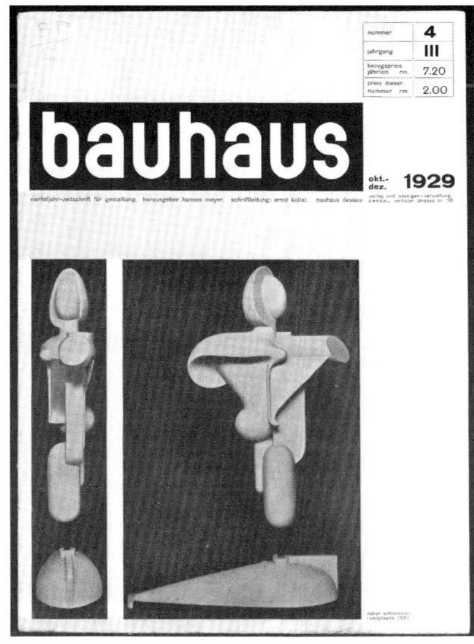

Joost Schmidt (1893–1948), designer,
Bauhaus Zeitschrift 4/III, 1929. Gift of Josef
Albers, BR49.42.11.

A large portion of the Bauhaus holdings is covered by the following categories:

Paintings. Paintings by Bauhaus masters, including Albers, Feininger, Kandinsky, Klee, Moholy-Nagy, Muche, Bayer, Schlemmer. Paintings by Bauhaus students including Hannes Beckmann, T. Lux Feininger, and Fritz Winter. Paintings by students studying in American schools based on the Bauhaus model — at Newcomb College, Black Mountain College (under the instruction of Josef Albers), and Brooklyn College.

Drawings. Drawings by Bauhaus masters, including Klee, Kandinsky, Itten, Feininger, Schlemmer, Moholy-Nagy, Bayer, and Albers, as well as by Bauhaus students, especially Bertrand Goldberg, Ludwig Hirschfeld-Mack (numerous color studies), and Max Preiffer-Watenphul, and by students studying in American schools based on the Bauhaus model.

Prints. Prints by Bauhaus faculty members, as well as most of the prints in the Bauhaus portfolios published under the direction of Lyonel Feininger; prints by Bauhaus students including Röhl, Schawinsky, and Baschant.

Sculpture. Moholy-Nagy's original *Light-Space Modulator* (1923–30), a sandblasted glass panel by Josef Albers, numerous works by Gerhard Marcks, Hannes Beckmann, and Max Bill, as well as by design students at Newcomb College.

Textiles. Large weavings, small samples, and some watercolor designs by Anni Albers, Gunta Stadler-Stölzl, Marli Ehrmann, Benita Otte, and Margarete Bittkow-Köhler. Eleven hundred small samples plus weaving instructions by Otti Berger.

Photographs. Photographs by Josef Albers, T. Lux Feininger, Howard Dearstyne, Herbert Bayer, Pius Pahl, and Erich Consemüller, among others,

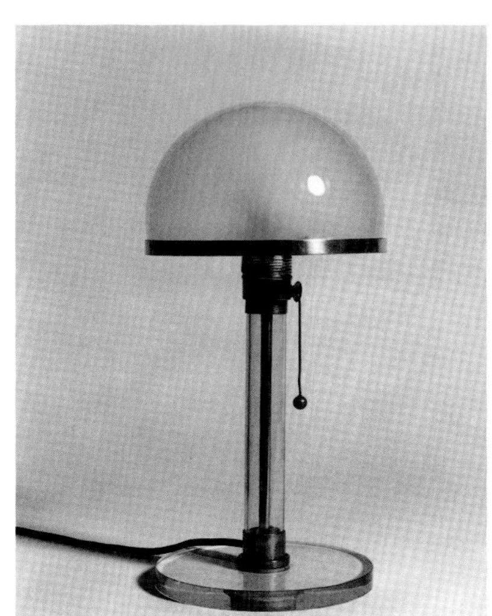

Karl Jucker (b.1902) and Wilhelm
Wagenfeld (1900–1990), Table Lamp,
1923–24. Glass base and stem with milk
glass shade, h. 36.2 cm. Gift of Walter
Gropius, BR49.248.

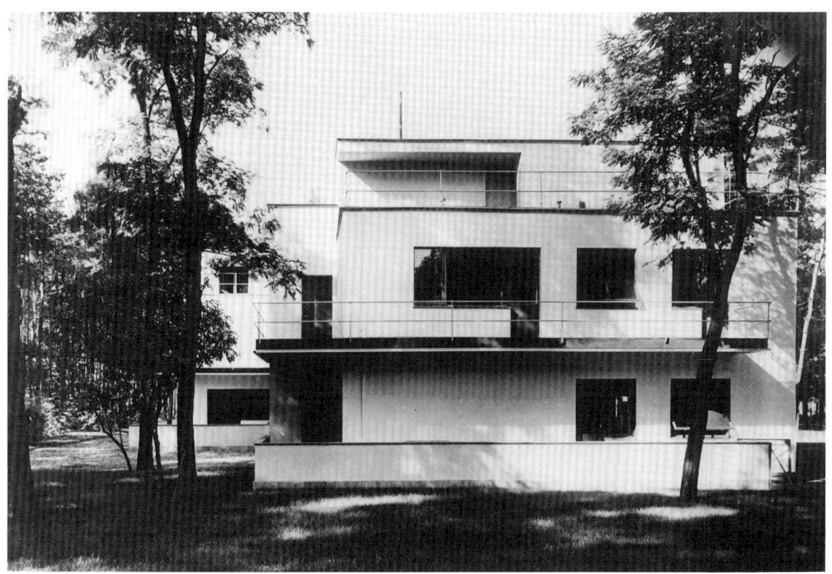

Lucia Moholy-Nagy (1894–1989), **Moholy-Nagy's Faculty House at Dessau,** *ca. 1926.* **Photograph, 65 x 93 cm. Gift of Walter Gropius, BRGA21.37.**

including many that document Bauhaus workshops and products.

Architecture. Numerous materials documenting Gropius's projects (see separate description). Various designs by Max Bill, Howard Dearstyne, Carl Fieger, Bertrand Goldberg, Mies van der Rohe, and Georg Muche.

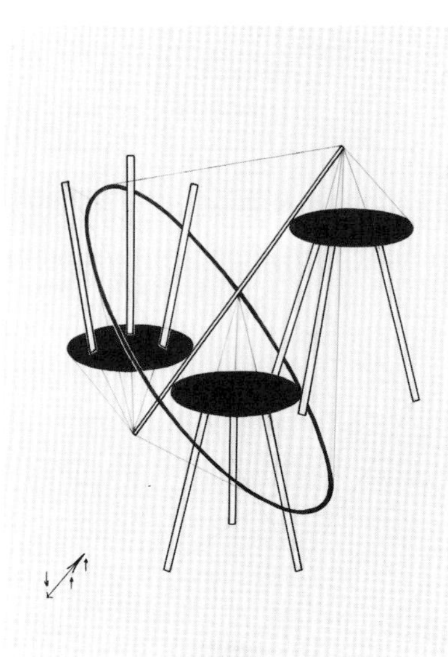

Howard Dearstyne (1903–79), **Bauhaus Analytical Exercise,** *ca. 1930.* **Graphite, black and colored inks, 28.5 x 22 cm. Gift of Marjorie Smolka, 1984.203.3**

Metalwork. Objects by Marianne Brandt, Karl Jucker, Wilhelm Wagenfeld, Josef Albers, Christian Dell, and Max Krajewski.

Woodwork. Two chess sets by Josef Hartwig.

Furniture. Tubular steel chairs and tables made by Marcel Breuer (and Mart Stam); Barcelona chairs designed by Mies van der Rohe.

Typography. Book, flyer, poster, and letterhead design by numerous Bauhaus faculty members, in particular Herbert Bayer; also Moholy-Nagy, Itten, Schlemmer, and Röhl. Sets of postcards advertising a 1923 exhibition; Bauhaus books; and Bauhaus newsletters. Also later typography by Herbert Bayer.

Ceramics. Pottery by Otto Lindig and a ceramic sculpture by Gerhard Marcks.

Wallpaper. Numerous samples and display books of Bauhaus-generated wallpaper, produced by the Hannoversche Tapetenfabrik/Gebr. Rasch company in the 1930s as well as after World War II. Some designed by Hinnerk Scheper and Josef Albers.

The Walter Gropius Archive

Over a twenty-year period, the architect donated some three thousand drawings, prints, and photographs documenting his architectural work from 1906 to 1946, when he founded The Architects Collaborative (TAC), as well as one later building on which he served as partner-in-charge. This generous gift has been supplemented by further important donations of photos, drawings, prints, books, and memorabilia from Boston's Institute of Contemporary Art, from Gropius's wife Ise and daughter Ati, and from TAC.

Around 1953, Gropius placed a large number of his architectural drawings, prints, and photographs on long-term loan to the museum. He donated them shortly before his death in 1969.

The result of these many gifts is that the Archive now holds documentation on 114 architectural and design projects between 1911 and 1946, and on one 1955–57 TAC project on which Gropius was partner-in-charge. This documentation consists of drawings, prints, photographs, space and cost estimates, and some building specifications. In addition, there is a 1938 model of the Gropius residence. Further photographic material includes hundreds of small documentary file photographs of architectural projects, color slides of the Gropius residence, slides from the architect's travels, photographs he used in exhibitions, and family photographs. Printed materials include volumes from Gropius's personal library, numerous pamphlets and magazines in German and English documenting his work and the Bauhaus, and newspaper clippings from the years after his death, especially on the occasion of the opening of the Bauhaus-Archiv in Berlin.

The Houghton Library contains Gropius correspondence after 1937, drafts of earlier speeches and articles, and photocopies of his earlier letters, the originals of which are at the Bauhaus-Archiv in Berlin. It also holds several boxes of press clippings, and Harvard's Lamont Library has fifteen microfilm reels of press notices from 1917 to 1961.

In 1980–81, the architectural component of the Archive was reorganized and catalogued by Professor

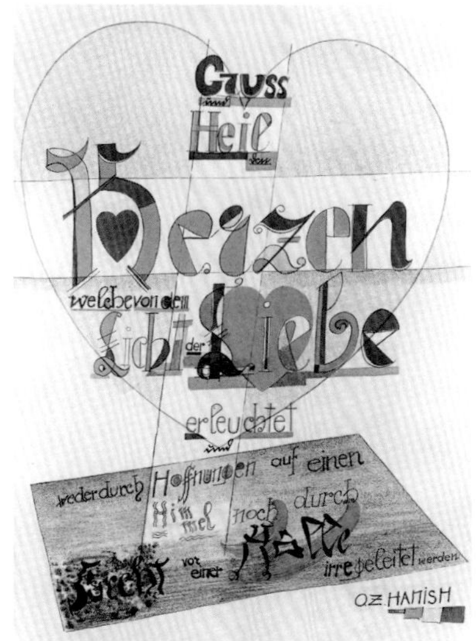

Johannes Itten (1888–1967), Proverb, 1921. Color lithograph, 29.5 x 23 cm. Gift of Julia Feininger, BR56.254.

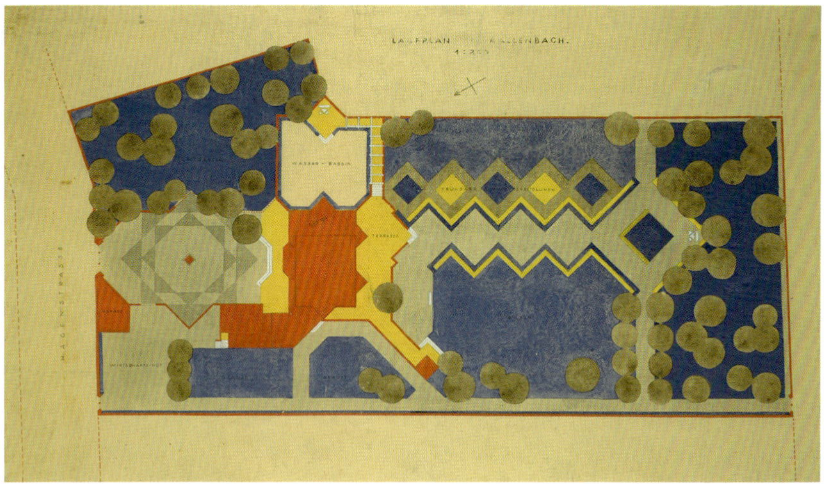

Walter Gropius (1883–1969), **Kallenbach Residence, ground plan,** *1921–22. Ink with colored washes, 44.8 x 75.4 cm. Gift of Walter Gropius, BRGA7.1.*

Winfried Nerdinger of Munich. This work culminated in 1985 in a major exhibition of 143 works, with accompanying scholarly catalogue, that traveled to the Bauhaus-Archiv in Berlin and the Deutsches Architekturmuseum in Frankfurt. The exhibition was appropriately dedicated to the memory of Charles L. Kuhn, who died in that year. In 1990, all the visual materials of the Gropius Archive at the Busch-Reisinger Museum were published by Garland Publishing in its Architectural Series. The three-volume series is accompanied by a fourth volume of projects completed while Gropius was at The Architects Collaborative.

The Lyonel Feininger Archive

Lyonel Feininger carefully preserved and precisely dated many of his working drawings. Thanks to the generosity of his widow and sons Lux and Andreas some 5,400 of these sketches were given to Harvard as part of a Feininger Archive. The Archive also contains finished and twelve unfinished paintings, numerous finished drawings of all periods (including some at the Fogg), many woodcuts, thirteen comic strips from *The Chicago Tribune* in 1906–7, numerous slides and photographs of travel, friends, and objects of interest, memorabilia, and documentary materials (including twenty diaries by Julia Feininger from 1938 to 1956 and 1960, documentary photographs of Feininger's works, books, magazine articles, and exhibition catalogues, etc.). In addition, thousands of letters were donated to the Busch-Reisinger Museum; these written materials are now on deposit in the Department of Manuscripts at Harvard's Houghton Library. Houghton also contains five hundred photographs taken by the artist. These gifts make Harvard the most important repository of the work of one of the century's major German-American artists.

The drawings span nearly sixty-five years — from 1892 to 1955, the year before Feininger's death — and give an extraordinary glimpse into the working

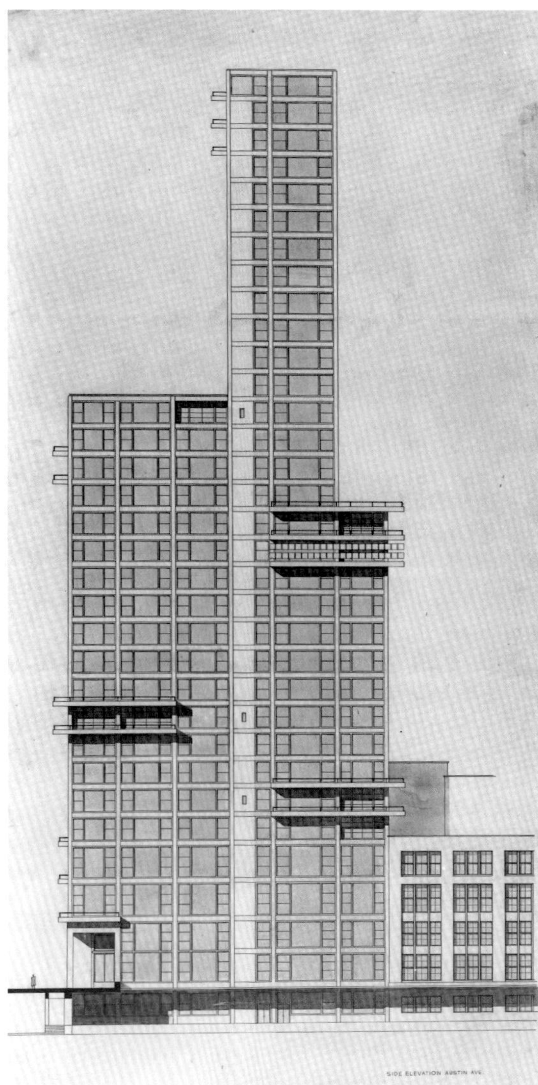

Walter Gropius (1883–1969), Design for the Chicago Tribune Competition, elevation, 1922. Ink, 152.4 x 76.2 cm. Gift of Walter Gropius, BRGA10.3.

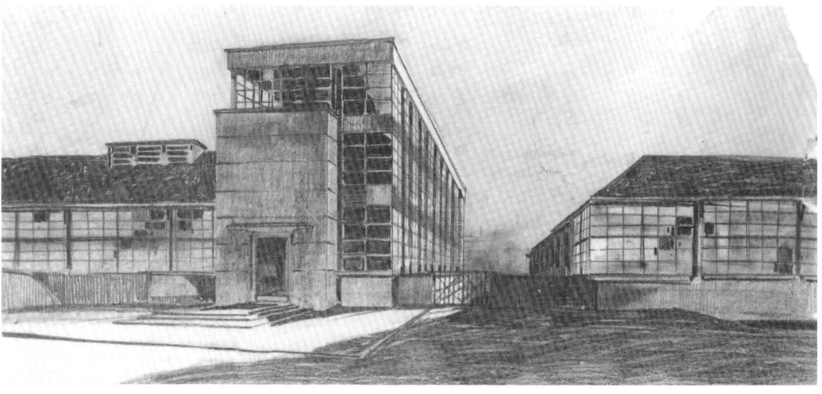

Walter Gropius (1883–1969), Fagus Shoe-Last Factory, perspective, 1910–11. Graphite with white wash, 40 x 60 cm. Gift of Walter Gropius, BRGA3.1.

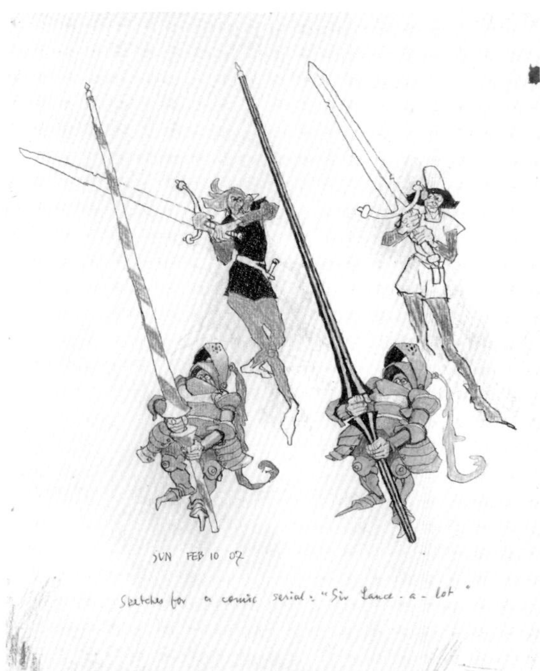

Lyonel Feininger (1871–1956), Sketches for a comic serial: Sir Lance-a-Lot, 1907. Ink and colored chalks with graphite, 30.8 x 23.7 cm. Gift of T. Lux Feininger, 1986.339.

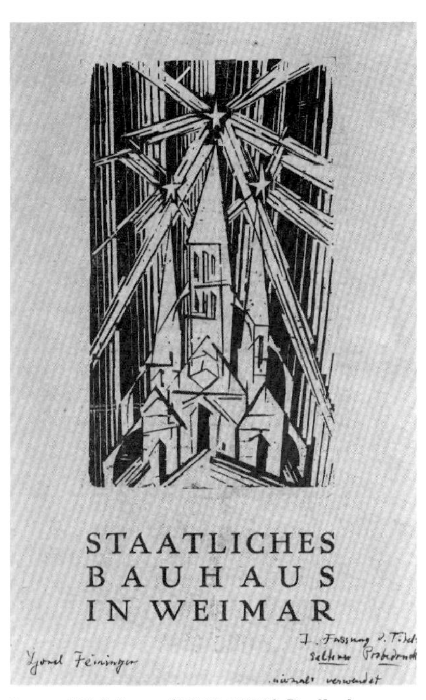

Lyonel Feininger (1871–1956), Preliminary design for cover to Bauhaus Proclamation, 1919. Woodcut with text, 31.6 x 19.4 cm. Gift of Julia Feininger, BR49.198.

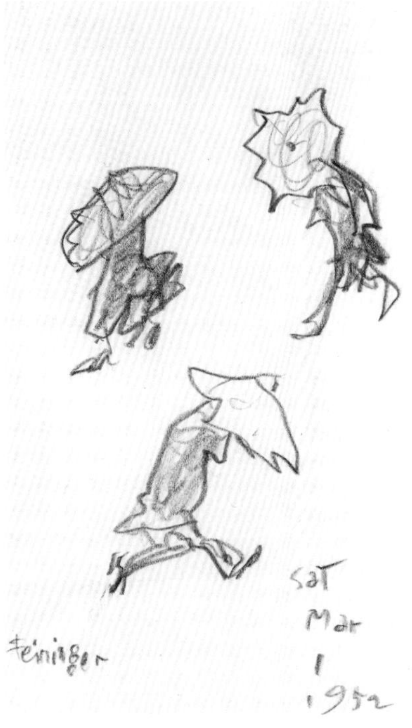

Lyonel Feininger (1871–1956), Figures Scurrying on a Rainy March Day, 1953. Graphite, 20.3 x 12.8 cm. Gift of Julia Feininger, BR63.3615.

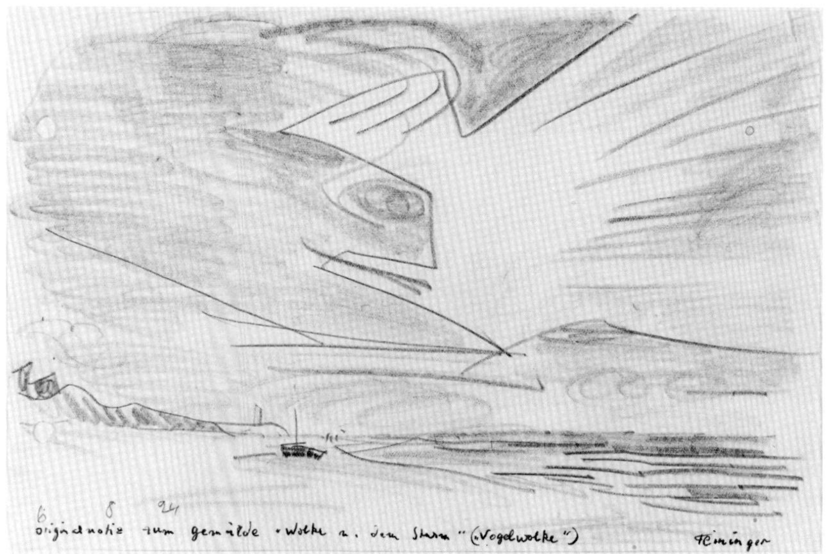

Lyonel Feininger (1871–1956), Sketch for Bird Cloud (see p. 61), 1924. Graphite, 14 x 21.5 cm. Gift of T. Lux Feininger, 1986.312.

methods of the artist. He called the sketches "nature notes" — *Naturnotizzen* — and the majority are indeed sketches from nature drawn on any scrap of paper at hand, with pencil, crayon, charcoal, or ink. Feininger often consulted his collection of "notes" and occasionally they would be used years later for his finished paintings.

The Postwar Collections

In his annual report for 1949–50, Kuhn wrote that "the artistic production of postwar Germany should be watched carefully and should be represented in the museum if it proves to be significant." Although the collection of German (and, of course, Austrian, Swiss, and related) postwar art has not yet achieved the level of concentrated quality which marks the holdings of early modernism, there is no doubt that Kuhn and subsequent curators have deemed contemporary art since 1945 sufficiently significant to be added in increasing quantity to the Busch-Reisinger.

The dynamic acquisitiveness of the 1950s extended to current production, with a special focus on the German variants of international abstractionism of those years. Together with acquisitions from the 1960s, the early 1970s, and a few from the 1980s, these acquisitions now amount to a well-rounded group of works by Baumeister, Werner, Trökes, Jaenisch, Hartung, Winter, Nay, Trier, Thieler, and Schumacher.

Kuhn did not abandon his predilection for sculpture, adding relatively traditional works by Marcks, Jaenisch, Forster, Heiliger (including one piece given by Mr. and Mrs. Max Wasserman), Koenig, Meier-Denninghof, and others. He was also open to less traditional forms of three-dimensional work, acquiring pieces by Schulze and Uecker in 1967. Postwar design, with the small exception of a few items such as posters, never featured in Kuhn's acquisitions, and it is still not clear to what

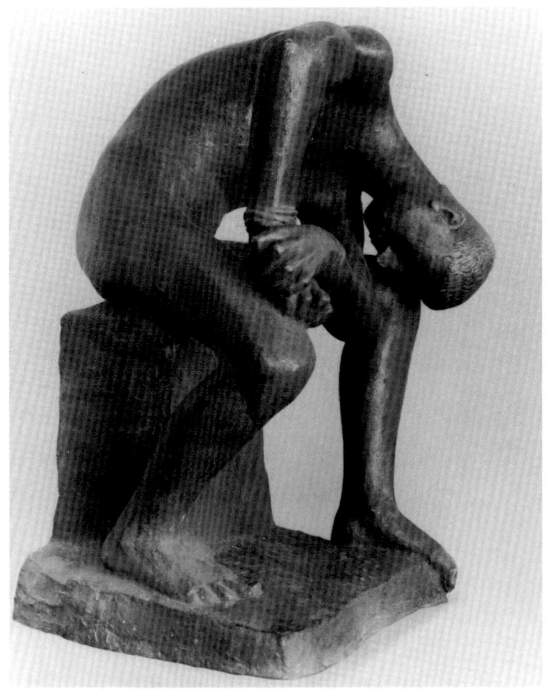

Gerhard Marcks (1889–1982), Prometheus II, *1948. Bronze, h. 78.1 cm. Museum purchase, BR52.71.*

extent the museum will attempt to extend its fine prewar holdings in this exciting field up to the present day.

As a whole, the 1970s did not see any sustained attempt to continue the momentum of acquiring contemporary art, even at the relatively reduced tempo of Kuhn's last years as curator. Works by several non-German artists entered the collection, including a Norwegian (Groth, given by Steingrim Laursen) and an Austrian (Rotterdam), though the high points were clearly major works by Marcks (once again), Lenk (1979), and Beuys (1978).

As the outlines of a possible future for the Busch-Reisinger became clearer during the 1980s, and as art from German-speaking Europe gained greater prominence on the world stage, a much more active program of contemporary art acquisitions was initiated. If the major focus of its public activities was to be modern art (say, from 1880 to 1980), the museum needed a suitably strong and useful postwar collection to match and merge with the famous earlier works. With the Fogg acquiring drawings and prints by Beuys, Baselitz, Richter, Polke, Kiefer, Penck, Disler, Blume, and others, the Busch-Reisinger added pieces by many of the same artists, and also by younger artists (such as Deistler, Buettner, Kiecol, and Odenbach). The museum has also begun systematically acquiring postwar German photography (including, so far, Steinert, Chargesheimer, Hallensleben, and Windstosser). Drawings (and works on paper in general) will no doubt emerge as a primary collecting interest (Otto Hall has been designed to reflect this), though the tradition of collecting sculpture will be respected (as with the 1980s acquisitions of pieces by Bernhard and Kricke).

Austrian art is now represented through a number of works by Rainer, while Swiss art has received particular attention. Building on Kuhn's acquisitions in the early 1960s of sculpture by Bodmer and Bill, the museum added a group of related works by Lohse and Graeser in the 1980s to make postwar geometric abstraction from Switzerland, with all its connections to the Bauhaus and related movements of the 1920s, a strong presence at Harvard.

The overall plan has been to solidify the representation of the period up to the end of the 1970s, either with major works by artists who came to maturity before then (as with paintings by Hoedicke, Antes, Richter, Klapheck, Graubner, and Uecker, acquired with substantial help from such patrons as Lufthansa German Airlines and the Cultural Council in the Federation of German Industry), or through an in-depth collection of drawings since 1945 (as with a substantial gift of such material, coordinated and given by the German Art Dealers' Association). It remains an important priority for the museum to acquire fine examples of art produced in the German Democratic Republic (1949–90)

As the decades recede, the museum must also be prepared for the possibility that the two halves of the century may begin to reveal important continuities, in such a way that art from the "hiatus" of 1933 to 1945 should be sought out and the collection hung to stress such a long view. Nevertheless, the museum remains committed to dealing with contemporary art on a regular basis, as the invigorating challenge of such material always deepens our understanding and appreciation of art from earlier periods.

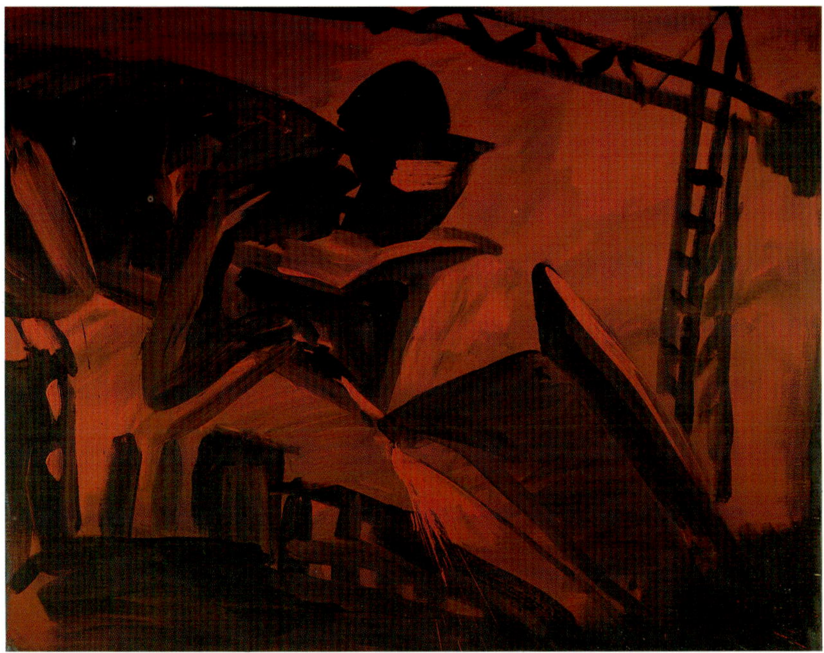

Karl Horst Hoedicke (b. 1938), Welder, 1978. Synthetic polymer, 155 x 189.9 cm. Gift of Friends of the Nationalgalerie, Berlin and European Friends of the Busch-Reisinger Museum, 1984.858.

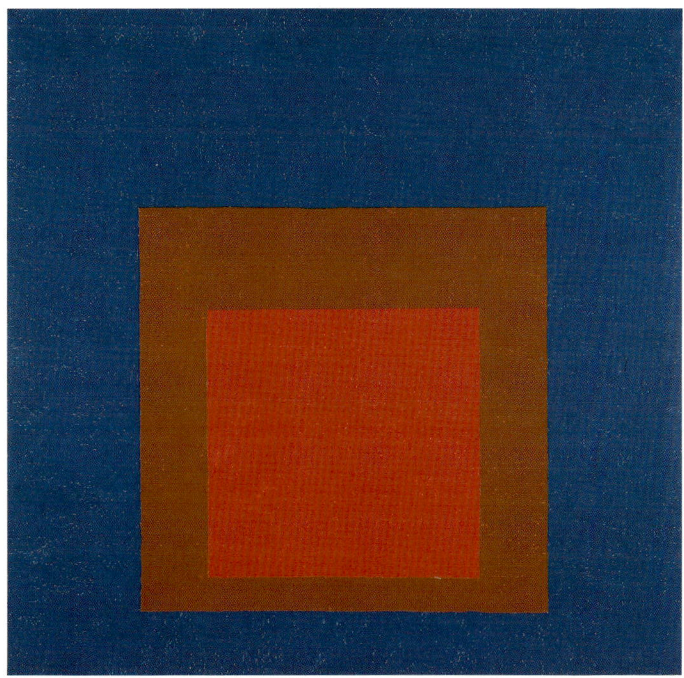

Josef Albers (1888–1976), Homage to the Square: Against Deep Blue, *1955. Oil on composition board, 61 x 61 cm. Anonymous gift, BR63.28.*

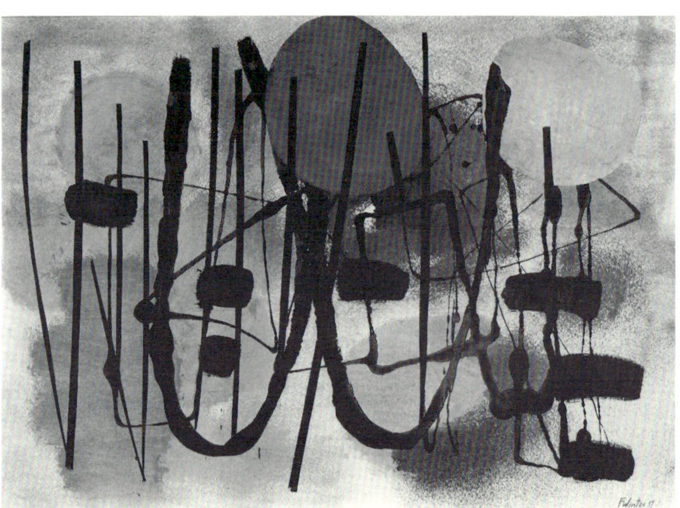

Fritz Winter (1905–76), Before Red, *1951. Oil on paper, 49.8 x 69.9 cm. Museum purchase, BR51.271.*

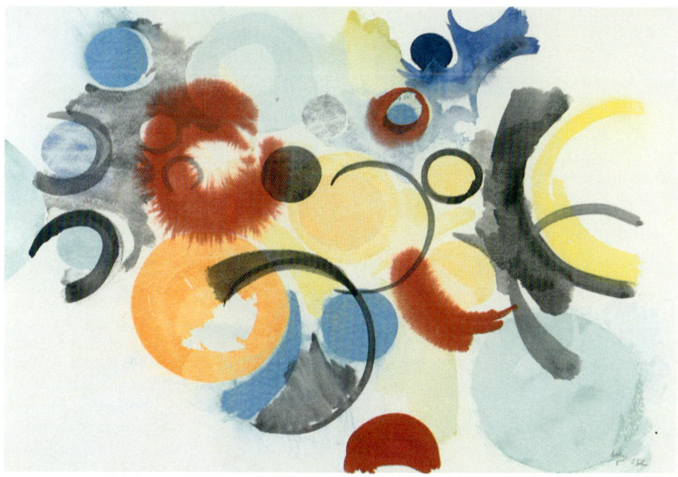

Ernst Wilhelm Nay (1902–68), Composition, 1957. Watercolor, 41.6 x 60 cm. Association Fund, BR57.31.

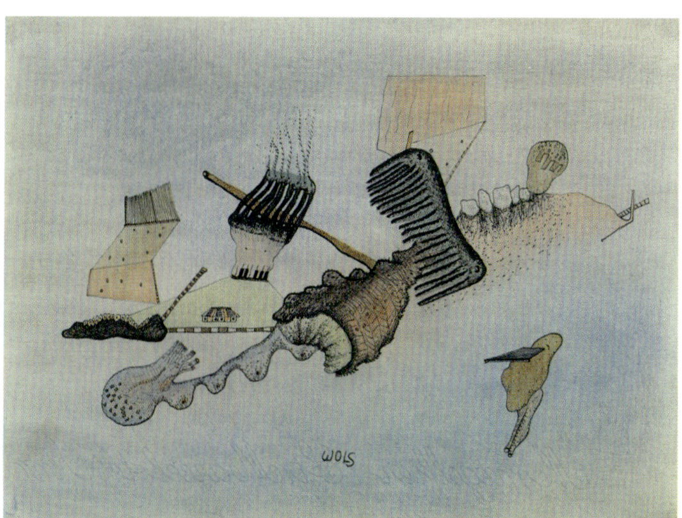

WOLS (Alfred Otto Wolfgang Schultze) (1913–51), Untitled, ca. 1939–40. Watercolor, 23.8 x 31.4 cm. Association Fund, BR59.39.

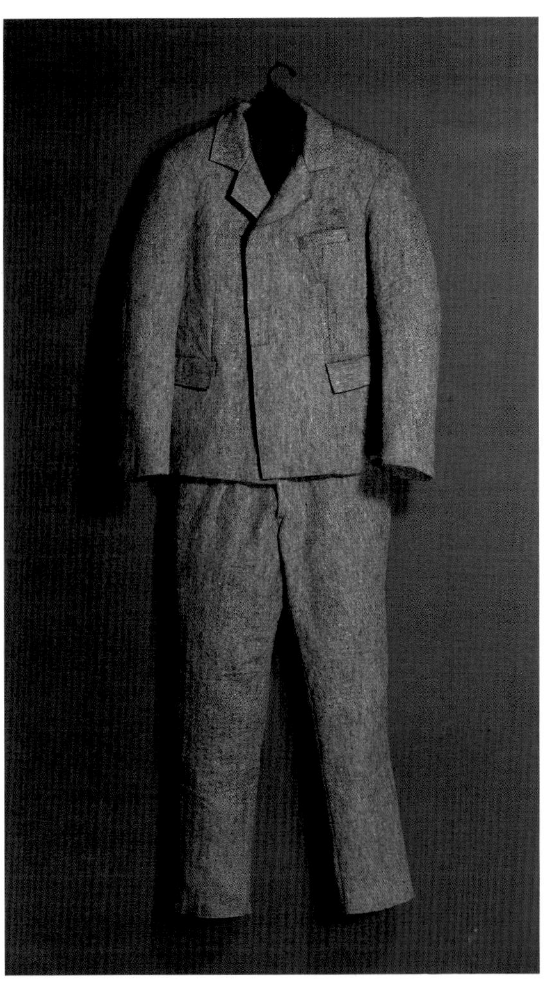

Josef Beuys (1921–86), Felt Suit, 1970, h. 170 cm. Purchase in memory of Eda K. Loeb, BR78.4.

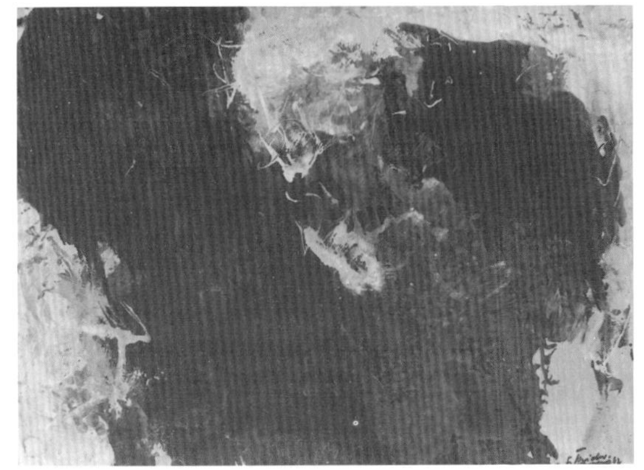

Fred Thieler (b. 1916), Untitled, 1962. Wash and gouache on paper mounted on board, 74.4 x 98.6 cm. (sight). Gift of Grundkreditbank, Berlin, 1985.348.

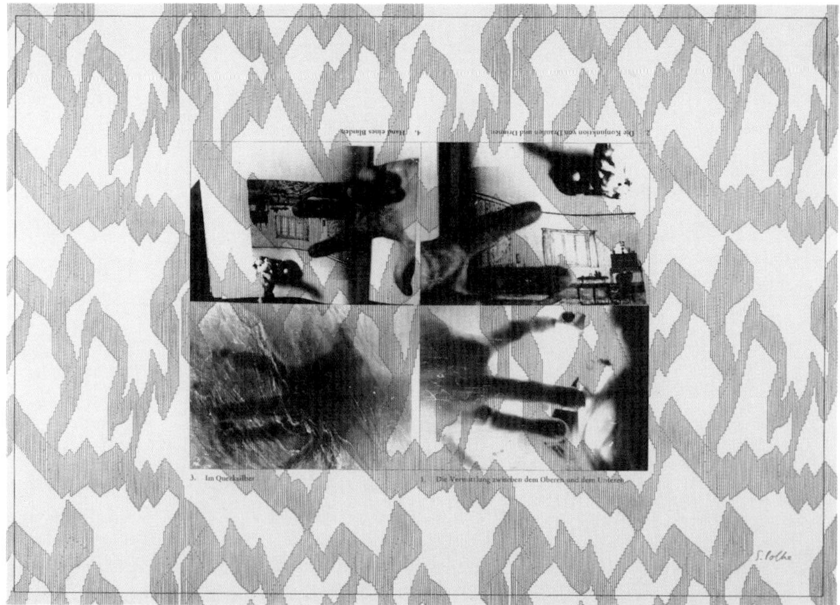

Sigmar Polke (b. 1941), Hands (The Mediation between the Upper and the Lower)*, 1973. Offset lithograph on paper with elephant skin pattern, 45.5 x 62.8 cm. Antonia Paepcke DuBrul Fund, 1989.53.*

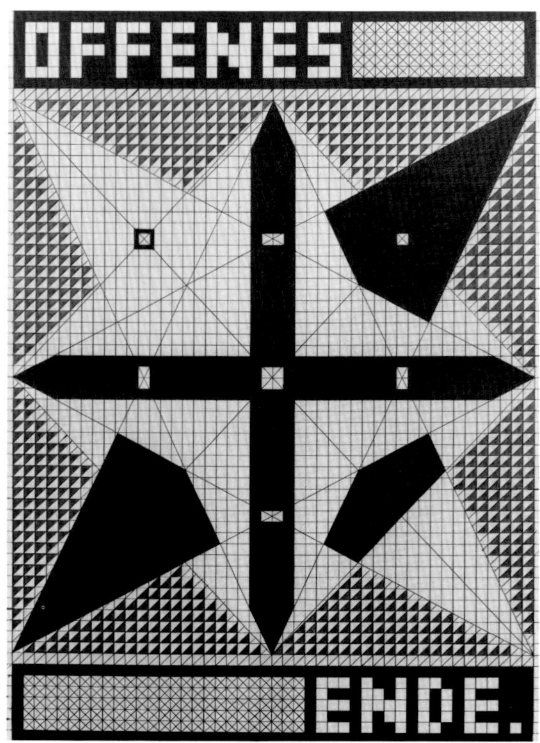

Michael Deistler (b. 1949), Open End, 1987. Colored inks, 68 x 48 cm. Museum purchase, 1988.433.

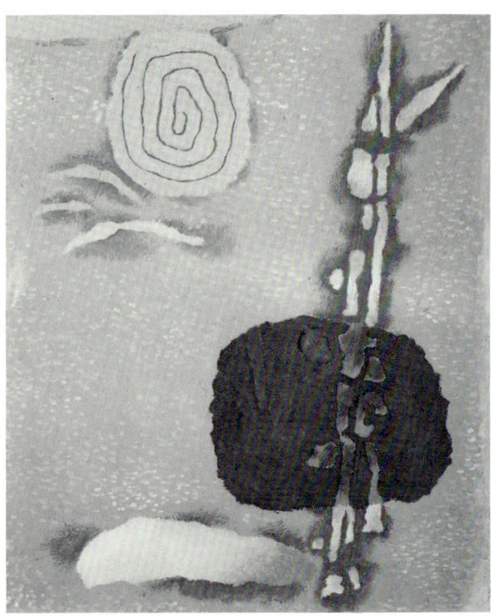

Willi Baumeister (1889–1955), Saffron Green with Red-Blue, *1955. Oil on composition board, 46 x 36.2 cm. Anonymous gift, BR56.39.*

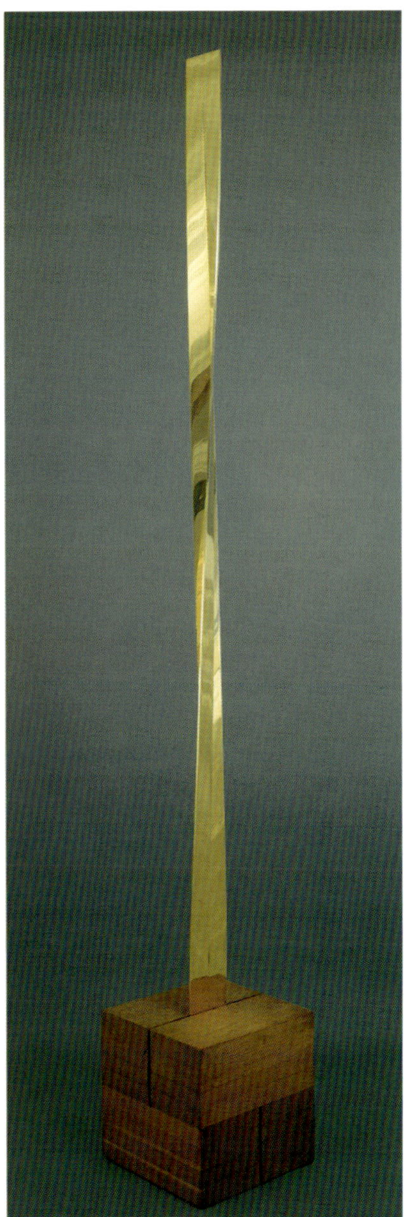

Max Bill (b. 1908), Endless Surface in Form of a Column, *1953–58. Gold-plated bronze, h. 250.2 cm. Gift of a group of friends of the museum, BR63.25.*

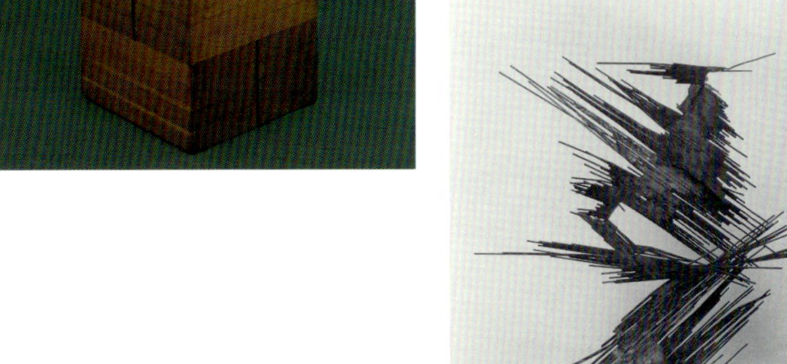

Norbert Kricke (1922–84), Space Sculpture, *ca. 1960. Welded wire, h. 55.5 cm. Gift of the Cultural Council in the Federation of German Industry in memory of its chairman, Berthold von Bohlen und Halbach, 1988.432.*

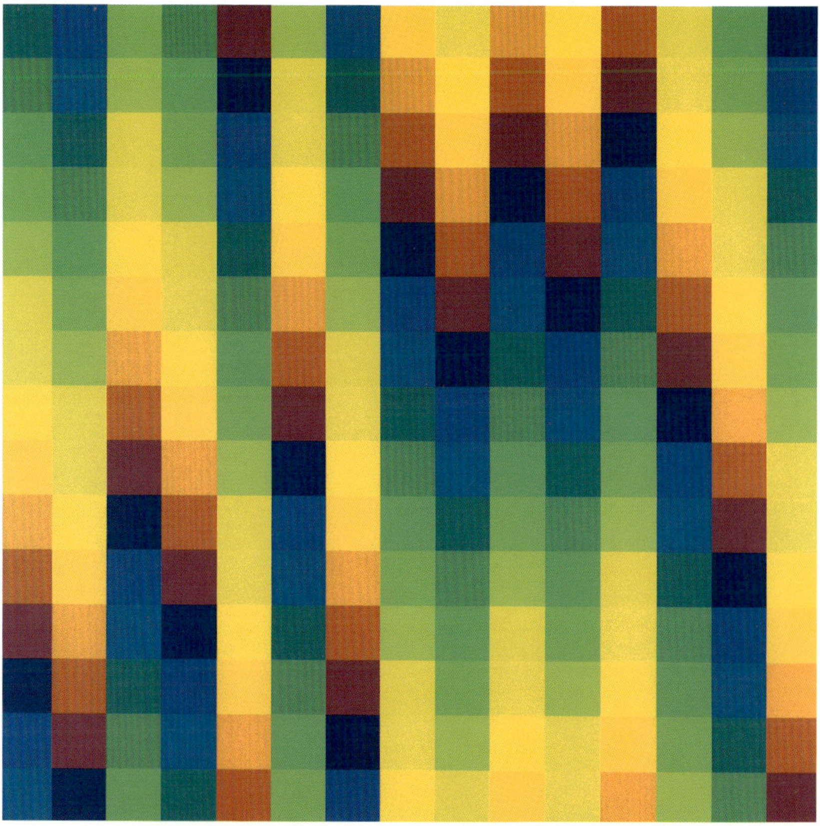

Richard Paul Lohse (1902–88), 15 Serial Rows of Equal Amounts of Color with Bright Emphasis, *1958/87. Acrylic, 150 x 150 cm. Gift of the Ernst Goehner Foundation and the Bank J. Vontobel & Co., 1987.28.*

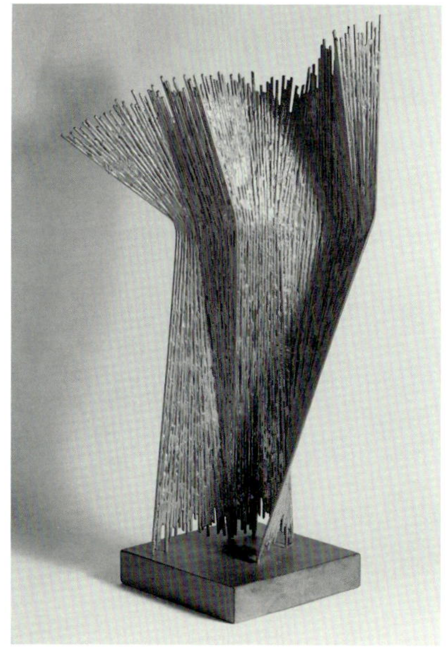

Brigitte Meier-Denninghoff (b. 1923), 61/6, *1961. Brass and pewter, h. 46.4 cm. Association Fund, BR61.112.*

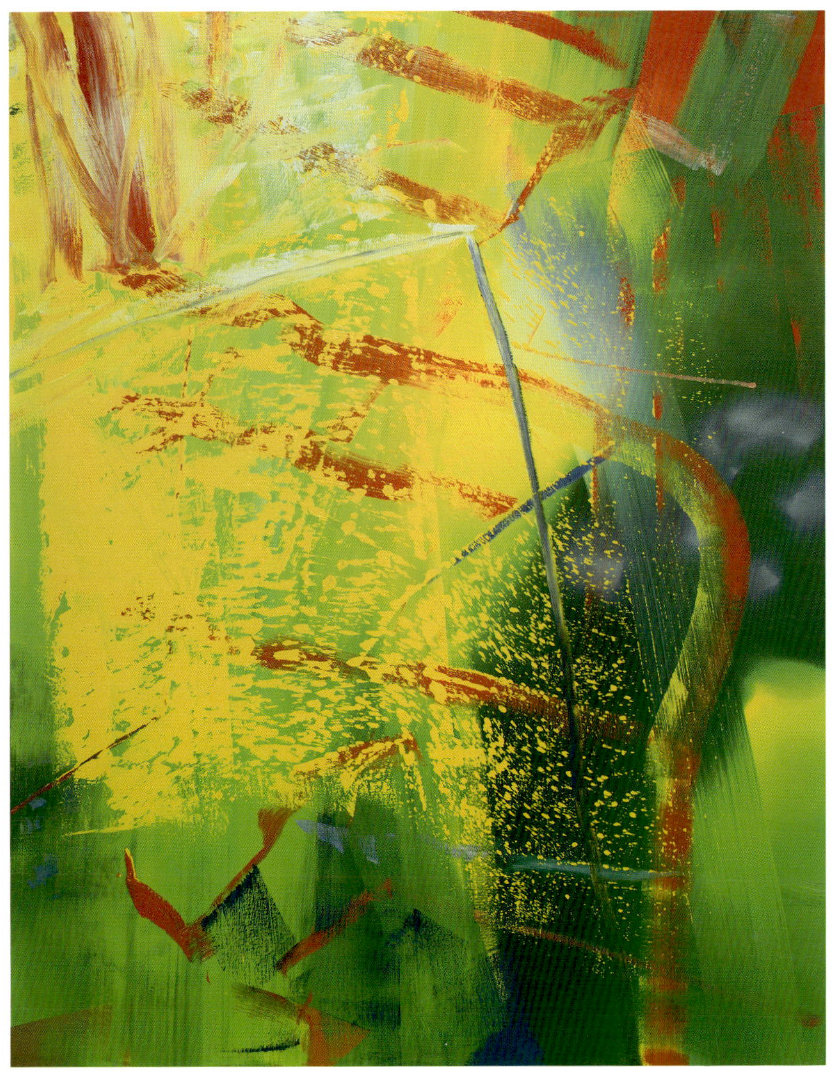

Gerhard Richter (b. 1932), Said, 1983. Acrylic, 260 x 200 cm. Gift of Lufthansa German Airlines, 1984.194.

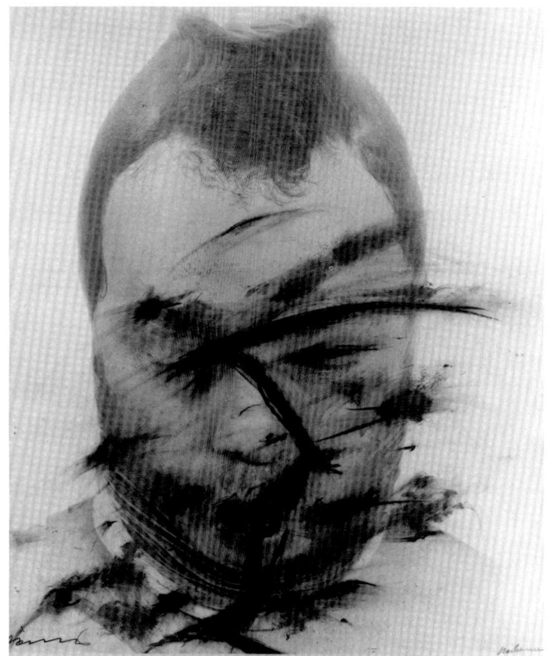

Arnulf Rainer (b. 1929), Face Farce, *1970–71. Photo reworked with charcoal, crayon, and acrylic, 60.4 x 50.5 cm. Museum purchase, 1986.3.*

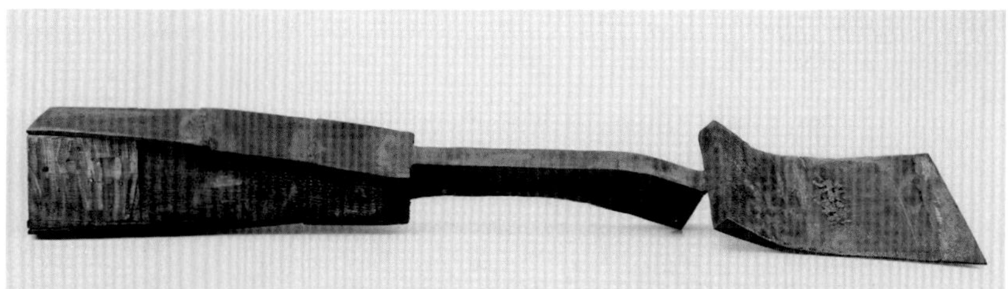

Franz Bernhard (b. 1934), In Three Parts, *ca. 1985. Iron and wood, l. 102.8 cm. Gift of Bogislav von Wentzel, 1987.27.*

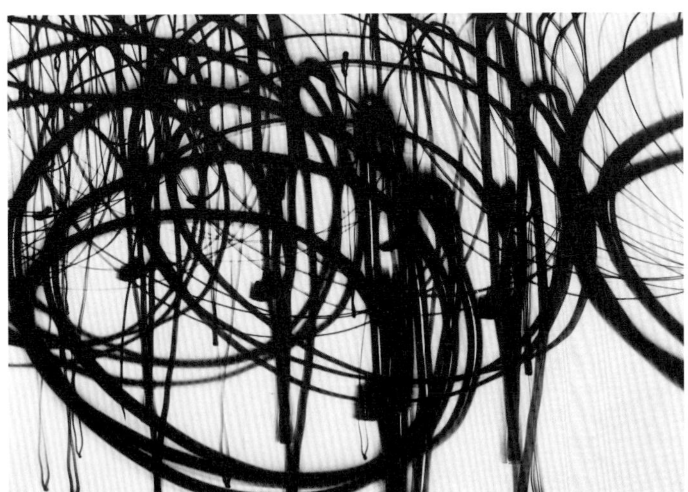

Otto Steinert (1915–78), Luminogram, 1952. Vintage silver print, 24.1 x 33.9 cm. Gift of the Cultural Council in the Federation of German Industry, 1991.52.

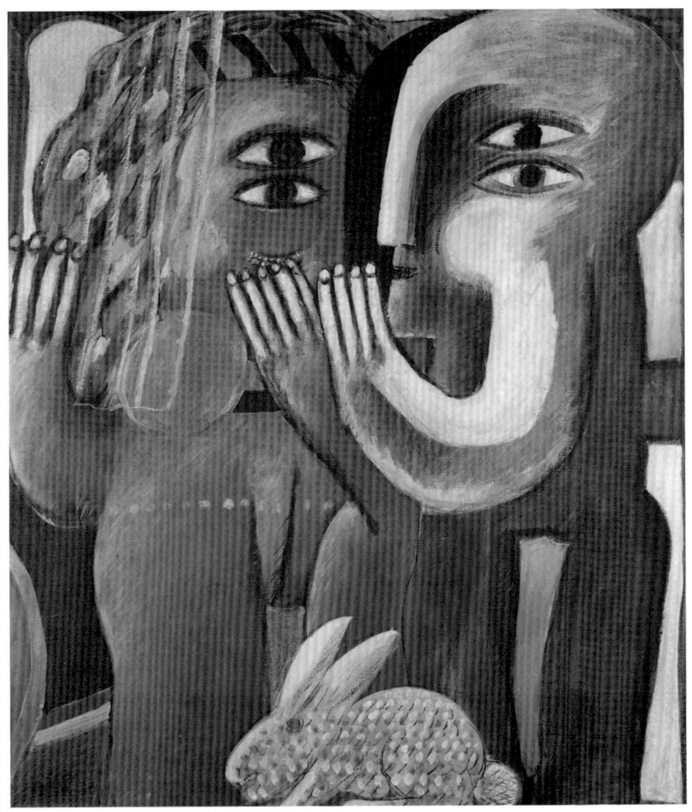

Horst Antes (b. 1936), Couple with Hare, 1962–64. Oil, 120 x 100 cm. Gift of the Cultural Council in the Federation of German Industry, 1988.421.

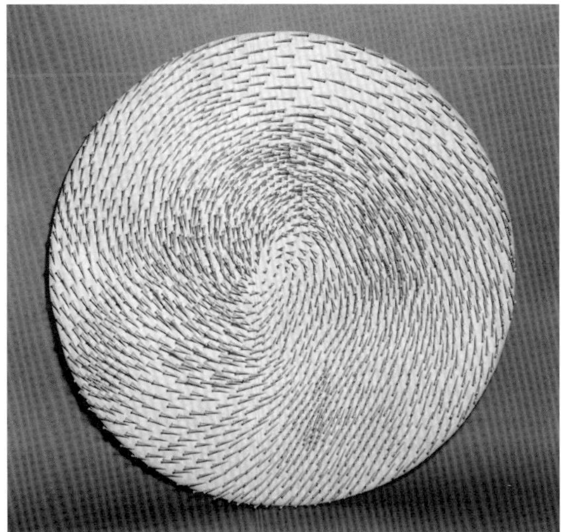

Gunther Uecker (b. 1930), Spiral White, ca. 1963. Wood, canvas, nails and paint, diam. 110.5 cm. Gift of the Cultural Council in the Federation of German Industry, 1985.23.

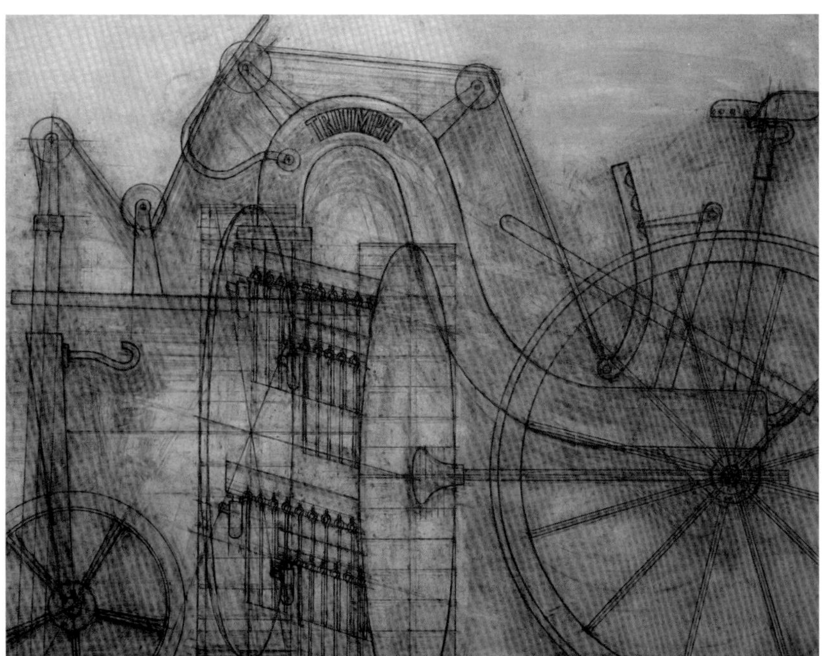

Konrad Klapheck (b. 1935), Sketch for Heldenlied, 1975. Charcoal with red pencil on yellow-gray prepared canvas, 224 x 281 cm. Gift of Lufthansa German Airlines, 1984.192.

List of Exhibitions, 1930–1991

This list comprises all exhibitions organized or presented by the Germanic/Busch-Reisinger Museum, as well as any others held at Adolphus Busch Hall. Installations under Kuno Francke were permanent, with no changes; Charles Kuhn instituted changing exhibitions.

The following abbreviations have been used:

c   =   catalogue
h   =   exclusively or to a large extent from Harvard collections
t   =   traveling show organized by Germanic/Busch-Reisinger Museum, followed by venues
★   =   information uncertain or not complete
org =   exhibition organizer, if other than Germanic/Busch-Reisinger Museum

January 15 – February 15, 1931
German Prints in Memory of Kuno Francke

March 25 – April 25, 1931
Dutch Drawings of the Seventeenth Century

Fall 1931
Contemporary Scandinavian and German Sculpture and Decorative Arts
h

January 15 – 29, 1932
Sculpture by Georg Kolbe

February 3 – 26, 1932
Modern Hungarian Paintings
org: College Art Association, New York

March 5 – 15, 1932
The Hundredth Anniversary of the Death of Johann Wolfgang von Goethe: Manuscripts, illustrated editions, and photographs of stage settings of Faust
h

May 4 – 26, 1932
Dutch Paintings of the Seventeenth Century
org: Detroit Art Institute and College Art Association, New York

October 10 – November 14, 1932
Swedish Peasant Wall Paintings
org: Art Institute of Chicago

November 17 – December 3, 1932
Entering the Twentieth Century/

GERMANIC MUSEUM

HARVARD UNIVERSITY

LOAN EXHIBITION OF

GERMAN PAINTING: "ENTERING THE TWENTIETH CENTURY"
ALSO
PAINTINGS BY MAX PECHSTEIN

NOVEMBER 17TH TO DECEMBER 3RD

THE PUBLIC IS CORDIALLY INVITED

1932 exhibition invitation

Paintings by Max Pechstein
org: College Art Association, New York

December, 1932 – January, 1933
International Photography
org: College Art Association, New York

February 3 – 18, 1933
Photographic Studies of Plant Forms by
Professor Karl Blossfeldt

February 23 – March 26, 1933
Reproductions of German Illuminated
Manuscripts
h

March 30 – April 30, 1933
Reproductions of German Renaissance
Drawings

June 1 – 11, 1933
Cambridge Public School Arts and Crafts

June 17 – August 17, 1933
Sculpture by Boston Artists

September 28 – October 15, 1933
Paintings by Ester Blomgren

November 4 – December 3, 1933
Painting and Sculpture by Scandinavian-
American Artists

January 6 – 26, 1934
Prints by Käthe Kollwitz: Studies from
the German Revolution 1919–21

February 9 – March 15, 1934
Modern German Ecclesiastical Art
org: Austrian Arts & Crafts Corp. for the
World's Fair Expo

April 10 – 29, 1934
Rembrandt Etchings and Drypoints
org: College Art Association, New York

May 5 – June 3, 1934
Sculpture and Drawings by Marta
Adams

June 6 – July 1, 1934
Paintings and Applied Arts by
Cambridge High School Students

October 10 – November 4, 1934
Oils and Water Colours by Carl Zerbe

December 4 – 22, 1934
International Advertising Posters
org: College Art Association, New York

February 1 – 25, 1935
Drawings by Modern German Sculptors
org: Curt Valentin

March 11 – April 11, 1935
Contemporary German Textiles
org: Marianne Willisch

October 15 – November 15, 1935
Graphic Art by Max Liebermann

October 30 – November 11, 1935
Bookbindings by Ignatz Wiemeler
org: Museum of Modern Art, New
York

November 22 – December 22, 1935
Watercolors and Drawings of George
Grosz

January 4 – February 4, 1936
Der Krieg: War Etchings by Otto Dix
org: Museum of Modern Art, New
York

February 6 – 27, 1936
Albrecht Dürer: Exhibition of
Engravings and Woodcuts from the
collection of Mr. Lessing Rosenwald
org: College Art Association, New York

February 1 – 25, 1936
Swedish Industrial Exhibition
org: College Art Association, New York

March 2 – 25, 1936
Swedish Glass: Exhibition of Orrefors
Glass
org: Blanche A. Byerley, New York

February 25★ – May 10, 1936
English Brass Rubbings

April 6★ – May 10, 1936
Watercolors by Christian Rohlfs
org: Detroit Institute of Arts

June 5 – September 30, 1936
Tercentenary Exhibition – German Art
from 1450–1550
c

October 22 – November 5, 1936
Reproductions of representative artists

from the early nineteenth century to the
present
h

November 9 – 30, 1936
Hubert Landau and Josef Albers

December 2 – 19, 1936
Paintings by Hans Boehler and Karl
Hofer
org: College Art Association, New York

December 21, 1936 – early 1937★
Lewis Rubenstein: Drawings and
Watercolors (at time of unveiling of
murals)

★1936 – 37
Rotating exhibition of paintings on
long-term loan by Pechstein, Marc,
Kandinsky, Kleinschmidt, Jawlensky,
Klee, Schmidt-Rottluff, Heckel, Nolde,
Campendonk, etc.

January 19 – February 6, 1937
Contemporary American Sculpture:
Gaston LaChaise, William Zorach, John
Flannagan, Alexander Calder
org: Boston Museum of Modern Art
(now the Institute of Contemporary Art)

March 1937
10 Watercolors by Frau Dodo Borchard-
Sattler

March 8 – 31, 1937
Paul Kleinschmidt
org: A. Goodman & Sons, Inc., New
York

April 5 – 24, 1937
Paintings by Wassily Kandinsky
org: College Art Association, New York

May 3 – 23, 1937
Paintings and Drawings by Friedrich
Springer

1936 – 37★
German Watercolors and Drawings of
the 19th and 20th centuries

November 8 – December 6, 1937
Work by German Children and
Unemployed
org: Nierendorf Galleries, New York

November 8 – December 6, 1937
German Graphic Art of the 15th and
16th Centuries

**December 15, 1937 – January 10,
1938★**
The Georg Jensen Collection of
Handwrought Silver
org: College Art Association, New York

January 10 – February 13, 1938
Lovis Corinth: Exhibition of Oils,
Watercolors, and Etchings
org: B. Westermann Co., Inc., New
York

March 21 – April 29, 1938
Modern German Sculpture: Kolbe,
Barlach, Lehmbruck, Sintenis, Marcks,
Belling, Fiori, Scheibe, Mataré, Karsh,
Haller

May 4 – June 1, 1938
Documentary Sketches by Lewis W.
Rubenstein: Drawings and Watercolors
of Life in an Arizona Mining Town, and
on the San Francisco Waterfront

Summer 1938
Watercolors and Drawings from the
Permanent Collection
h

December 1938
Christmas Theme in Woodcuts and
Engravings by German Artists of the
15th and 16th centuries

February 14 – March 13, 1940
Eighteenth Century Book Illustrations

from the Faber du Faur Library and the
Philip Hofer Collection

February 28 – March 27, 1940
Oils and Watercolors by Paul Klee

1939 – 40
Two exhibitions of framed colored
reproductions for Fine Arts courses.

April 1940
Fritz Pfeiffer
org: Massachusetts WPA

November 12 – December 7, 1940
Paintings by Max Beckmann

December 23, 1940 – January 29, 1941
Book Illustrations and Drawings of the
Romantic Period in Germany

February 4 – March 4, 1941
Paintings by Franz Marc
org: Buchholz Gallery

1940 – 41★
Art Collected by Undergraduate
Students

March 10 – April 10, 1941
Exhibition of Harvard-Radcliffe Student
Art

April 10 – 25, 1941
Books by Rainer Maria Rilke
h

September 20 – October 21, 1941
Stockholm Builds: Photos of Modern
Swedish Architecture
org: Museum of Modern Art, New
York

January 5 – 26, 1942
George Grosz: A Comprehensive
Exhibition of his Oils, Watercolors,
Drawings and Prints
c, org: Museum of Modern Art, New
York

April 6 – May 6, 1942
Paintings, Drawings, and Etchings by
Paul Wieghardt and Sculpture by Nelli
Bar

May 26 – June 26, 1942
Paintings by Members of the
Massachusetts Art Project
org: Works Projects Administration Art
Program, Federal Works Agency

Spring 1945★
Annual Exhibition of the Cambridge Art
Association

Spring 1946★
Annual Exhibition of the Cambridge Art
Association

Spring 1947★
Annual Exhibition of the Cambridge Art
Association

Spring 1948★
Annual Exhibition of the Cambridge Art
Association

July 5 – September 3, 1948
German Sculpture, Painting, Drawing
(1920–33)

October 1 – 29, 1948
Kaethe Kollwitz: Prints, Drawings,
Sculpture
t, Wells College, Aurora, N.Y.; Galerie
St. Etienne, New York

October 1 – 20★, 1948
Marcel Breuer: Architect and Designer
org: Museum of Modern Art, New
York

November 3 – 26, 1948
Modern German Paintings, Sculpture
and Decorative Art
h

December 6, 1948 – January 7, 1949
Max Beckmann: Paintings
org: City Art Museum of St. Louis

January 11 – February 10, 1949
North European Painting of the
Fifteenth and Sixteenth Centuries in
Reproduction
h

February 14 – March 7, 1949
Mies van der Rohe
org: Museum of Modern Art, New
York

March 15 – April 15, 1949
Creative Design and the Consumer
org: Phillips Andover Academy,
Andover, Mass.

March 15 – April 15, 1949
Graphic Art by Bauhaus Masters
h

Spring 1949★
Annual Exhibition of the Cambridge
Art Association

May 16 – June 11, 1949
Children's Art from Two Greater
Boston Red Feather Agencies

June 20 – August 3, 1949
Modern Painting, Sculpture, Graphic
Art and Industrial Design
org: Société Anonyme, Yale University
Art Gallery, New Haven, Conn.

September 28 – November 3, 1949
Art of Goethe's Time, in
Commemoration of the 200th
Anniversary of His Birth

November 14 – December 20, 1949
George Grosz, A Piece of My World:
Paintings and Drawings of Social Satire

January 3, 1949 – February 4, 1950
Textiles by Black Mountain Students/
Lobmeyr Glass/Modern Painting and
Graphic Arts (first two loan shows; third
from permanent collection)

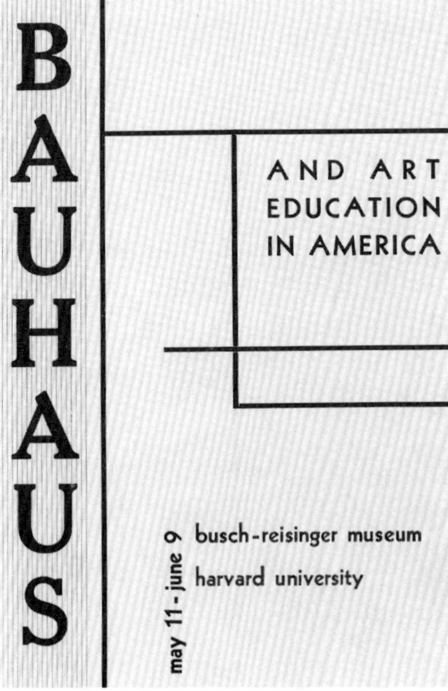

1951 Bauhaus exhibition poster

February 6 – 27, 1950
Laszlo Moholy-Nagy
Jointly organized with Harvard School
of Design and MIT School of
Architecture

March 8 – April 3, 1950
Paul Klee: Paintings and Prints
org: Museum of Modern Art, New
York

April 17 – May 2, 1950
Annual Exhibition of the Cambridge
Art Association

May 8 – June 22, 1950
German Old Masters Prints and
Drawings
h

Fall 1950
Modern German Sculpture and
Painting
h

October 3 – 31, 1950
Textiles by Anni Albers

org: Museum of Modern Art, New
York

November 2 – 30, 1950
Graphic Art by Hendrik Nicolaas
Werkman
org: American Federation of the Arts

December 8, 1950 – January 12, 1951
Kirchner: First American Retrospective
Exhibition of Oils, Watercolors, Prints
c

January 22 – March 4, 1951
Artists of the Graduate Center: Albers,
Arp, Bayer, Kepes, Lippold, Miro

March 12 – 27, 1951
Annual Exhibition of the Cambridge Art
Association

April 1 – 22, 1951
Saints in Gothic Art
org: The American Federation of Arts

April 1 – May 5, 1951
An Exhibition of Twentieth Century
Drawings and Watercolors from the
Collection of Mr. and Mrs. Richard S.
Davis

1950 – 51
A series of changing exhibits of
illustrated books and other materials
Department of German Languages and
Literature, Harvard University
h

May 11 – June 9, 1951
The Bauhaus and Art Education in
America
h, org: Harvard Museum Training
Course students

July – September, 1951
Modern Painting and Sculpture: The Art
of the Bauhaus
h

October 3 – 24, 1951
Vincent Van Gogh, Artist: An
Interpretive Exhibition
org: Art Institute of Chicago and the
American Federation of Arts

November 2 – 24, 1951
Harvard Art Association

November 30 – December 20, 1951
Carvers, Modelers, Welders
org: Museum of Modern Art, New
York

January 2 – February 4, 1952
Gropius, Architect and Teacher/The
Bauhaus Artists: Albers, Bayer,
Feininger, Kandinsky, Klee, Marcks,
Moholy-Nagy, Schlemmer
org: Busch-Reisinger and Institute of
Contemporary Art, Boston

February 13 – March 13, 1952
Ensor: Prints and Drawings
c, org: Museum of Modern Art, New
York

March 24 – April 12, 1952
Annual Exhibition of the Cambridge
Art Association

Spring 1952
Ballet Costumes by Oscar Schlemmer

April 16 – May 1, 1952
Museum Treasure Hunt: Works by
School Children of Greater Boston

May 9 – June 19, 1952
Dürer Before and After: German
Graphic Art XV and XVI Centuries
org: Harvard Museum Training Course
students

July – August 1952
Medieval Stained Glass

October 1 – 22, 1952
Contemporary Berlin Artists
org: The American Federation of Arts

October 29 – November 19, 1952
Paintings by Swedish Children
org: Museum of Modern Art, New
York

November 8 – December 20, 1952
Swedish Peasant Art and Modern
Swedish Industrial Design
c

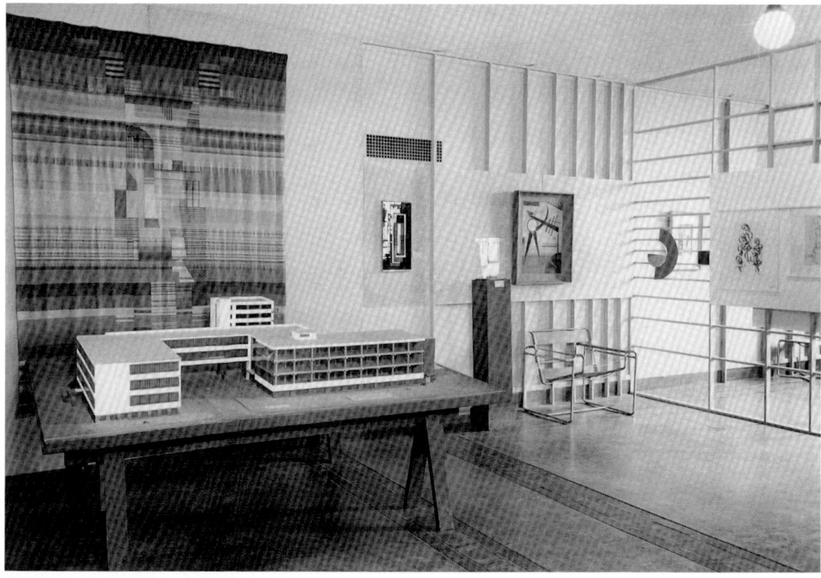

Bauhaus exhibition (1951)

December 27, 1952 – January 30, 1953
Modern German Painting, Sculpture, Decorative Arts
org: Harvard Museum Training Course students
h

February 8 – March 8, 1953
Contemporary Swiss Painting
org: Smithsonian Institution, Washington, D.C.

March 16 – April 11, 1953
Annual Exhibition of the Cambridge Art Association

April 18 – May 20, 1953
Exoticism in French Art: from Rococo to Impressionism
org: Harvard Museum Training Course students

June 1 – October 7, 1953
Modern German Painting and Sculpture
h

October 31 – November 28, 1953
Post-war Posters from Austria, Germany, Holland, Switzerland
org: Museum of Modern Art, New York

November 2 – 28, 1953
Exhibition of New Acquisitions: The Arthur Kraft Collection of German Impressionist Paintings and Drawings
h

December 3 – 31, 1953
Pennsylvania German Arts and Crafts
org: Smithsonian Institution, Washington, D.C.

December 10 – April 10, 1954
Art at the Bauhaus
h

January 8 – February 6, 1954
Color Prints in Postwar Germany
org: American Federation of the Arts

February 12 – March 20, 1954
Impressionism and Expressionism
org: Harvard Museum Training Course students

March 27 – April 17, 1954
Annual Exhibition of the Cambridge Art Association

April 20 – May 25, 1954
Design in Contemporary Textiles
org: Harvard Museum Training Course students

April 26 – May 25, 1954
Selection of Recent Acquisitions
h

April 26 – May 20, 1954
William Babcock: Painting and Drawings
org: Harvard Museum Training Course students

Summer 1954
Modern German Painting and Sculpture
h

Summer 1954
Art at the Bauhaus
h

November 1 – December 1, 1954
Graphic Works by Artists of the Bauhaus
h

December 8, 1954 – January 13, 1955
Selection of New Acquisitions of 1954: Modern German Sculpture and Painting
h

January 21 – February 26, 1955
Artists of the Blaue Reiter: Paintings
from 1920 to 1915 by Campendonk,
Jawlenski, Kandinsky, Feininger, Kubin,
Macke, Marc, and Klee
org: Busch-Reisinger and Valentin
Gallery, New York

March 7 – 26, 1955
Paintings by Prince Eugen of Sweden
org: The American Scandinavian
Foundation, New York

March 7 – April 2, 1955
Modern German Painting and
Sculpture
h

April 11 – 30, 1955
Annual Exhibition of the Cambridge
Art Association

May 9 – June 8, 1955
The Arts of Matisse
org: Harvard Museum Training Course
students

June 13 – July 1, 1955
Lewis Rubenstein: Paintings–
Drawings–Prints

July 5 – October 10, 1955
Modern German Painting, Sculpture
and Industrial Art
h

October 1 – November 7, 1955
German Expressionism and Abstract Art
h

October – November, 1955
Industrial Art of Germany, Holland and
Sweden
h

November 20 – December 20, 1955
Nuremberg and the German World:
German Graphic Art of the XVth and
XVIth Centuries
org: The American Federation of Arts

January 2 – February 11, 1956
Acquisitions of 1955
h

early 1956★
Modern German Art from the
Collection of the Museum
h

February 20 – March 10, 1956
Annual Exhibition of the Cambridge Art
Association

March 17 – April 15, 1956
Ernst Barlach Retrospective Exhibition:
Sculpture, Drawings, and Prints
c, org: Norman Geske and Naomi
Jackson

May 14 – June 16, 1956
Bauhaus in Germany and America
h, org: Harvard Museum Training
Course students

Summer 1956
German Painting, Sculpture, and
Industrial Design of the Twentieth
Century
h

October 3 – 25, 1956
Mid Century Revue: German
Watercolors, Drawings and Prints 1905–
1955
c, org: American Federation of Arts

November 6 – December 4, 1956
The Graphic Art of Kirchner and Nolde
org: Museum of Modern Art, New
York

December 10, 1956 – January 17, 1957
Lucas Van Leyden & Pieter Brueghel:
drawings and prints
h

December 10, 1956 – January 17, 1957
Acquisitions of 1956: 16th to 18th
centuries
h

January 24 – February 23, 1957
Recent Acquisitions: 20th Century
h

March 4 – April 6, 1957
War and its Aftermath: 1914–1925

Spring 1957
Annual Exhibition of the Cambridge
Art Association

May 13 – June 8, 1957
Modern German Art/Slavic Folk Art
h

Summer 1957
Modern German Art
h

October 15 – November 16, 1957
Twelve Scandinavian Designers
c, org: Smithsonian Institution,
Washington, D.C.

November 25 – December 30, 1957
Modern German Art at Harvard: Part I,
1900–1915
h

January 8 – February 8, 1958
Great Masters of Graphic Art: Dürer
and His Time
h

February 14 – March 22, 1958
Recent Acquisitions: XV–XX
Centuries
h

March 31 – April 19, 1958
Annual Exhibition of the Cambridge
Art Association

April 26 – June 14, 1958
Modern German Art at Harvard: Part
II, 1916–1957
h

June 18 – August 22, 1958
Modern German Sculpture, Painting,
and Industrial Art
h

October 6 – November 8, 1958
Lyonel Feininger: Paintings of Harbors,
Ships and the Sea
c

November 18 – December 20, 1958
Lovis Corinth 100th Anniversary
Exhibition: Watercolors and Drawings
c

December 23, 1958 – January 29, 1959
Albrecht Dürer: Masterpieces of
Graphic Art
h

January 1959
German Art, 1880 – present
h

February 3 – 23, 1959
The Baroque Illusion: Stage Designs,
1660–1850
org: American Federation of the Arts

March 8 – 28, 1959
Annual Exhibition of the Cambridge
Art Association

April 2 – May 3, 1959
Romanticism to Naturalism: German
Drawings and Prints of the Nineteenth
Century
h

May 11 – June 12, 1959
Aspects of Art Nouveau
org: Harvard Museum Training Course
students

June 2 – September 4, 1959
Old Masters and Modern Art from the
Collection of Edward M.M. Warburg/
Modern German Painting and
Sculpture

October 5 – November 7, 1959
Masterpieces of Modern German Art

from Harvard's Collections
h

November 16 – December 26, 1959
Modern German Graphic Art in
Memory of Louis W. Black
c, org: DeCordova Museum, Lincoln,
Mass., with the Busch-Reisinger

January 11 – February 13, 1960
New Acquisitions: Sculpture, Paintings,
Prints, and Decorative Art from the
Middle Ages to the Present
h

March 1960
Drawings of the Nineteenth Century
h

March 20 – April 6, 1960
Annual Exhibition of the Cambridge
Art Association

April 1960
Die Brücke
h

May 13 – June 8, 1960
A Hundred Years of English Landscape
Drawing 1750–1850
c, org: Harvard Museum Training
Course students

May 13 – June 8, 1960
Gustave Moreau and Adolphe
Monticelli
c, org: Harvard Museum Training
Course students

June 13 – September 2, 1960
Works of Paul Klee from Private and
Public Collections

October 3 – November 19, 1960
Reality and Imagination: A Century of
German Art, 1860–1960
h

November 28, 1960 – January 28, 1961
German Graphic Art from the Late

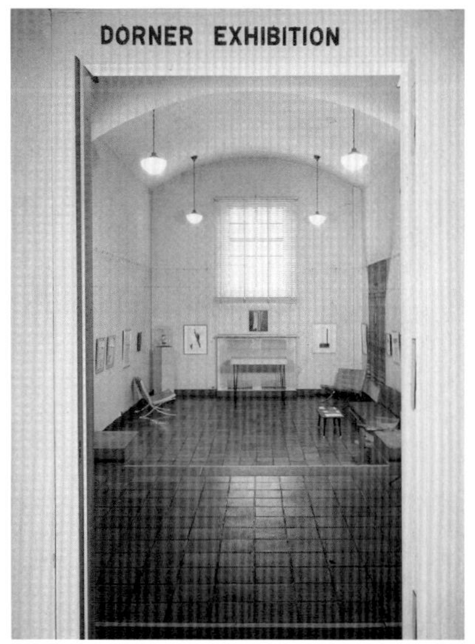

Exhibition of Dorner gifts, 1961

Middle Ages to the Reformation
h

March 23 – May 1, 1961
XXth Century Germanic Art from
Private Collections in Greater Boston
c

May 12 – June 30, 1961
Design and Structure in Modern
German Art: Gifts from the Collection
of Alexander and Lydia Dorner
h

October 3 – November 14, 1961
Artists of the Bauhaus: Painting,
Sculpture, Industrial Design
h

October 3 – November 14, 1961
German Art, 1900Ù–1960: Examples
from the Museum's Collections
h

**November 20, 1961 – January 8,
1962**
Pictorial Reflections of Drama:
Hauptmann to Barlach
h

February 19 – March 24, 1962
T. Lux Feininger: Paintings, Drawings,
Watercolors

April 25 – June 16, 1962
Rivers and Seas: Changing Attitude
Toward Landscape (1700–1962)
c, org: Harvard Museum Training
Course students

April 8 – June 15, 1962★
The Graphic Art of Schongauer and
Dürer
h

August 1962
German Art, 1860–1960
h

Summer 1962
Lyonel Feininger: 10 Paintings

October 1 – 31, 1962
Contemporary German Color Prints
org: Smithsonian Institution,
Washington, D.C.

**November 5, 1962 – January 7,
1963**
Artists of the "Brücke" – Graphic Art
h

February 4 – March 15, 1963
Recent Acquisitions: Works of Art
from the XVth to XXth Centuries
h

March 20 – April 16, 1963
The Intimate World of Lyonel
Feininger
org: Museum of Modern Art, New
York

May 18 – June 15, 1963
Walter Gropius: Architect, Creator,
Educator: for his 80th Birthday
org: Bauhaus Archive, Darmstadt

1963 – 64
Three Small Exhibits, including
Expressionist Prints★

February 24 – April 4, 1964
The Working Methods of Lyonel
Feininger: Selections from His Archives
h

October 13 – November 28, 1964
Sculpture, Decorative Arts, Painting:
XVIth–XXth Century
h

March 15 – May 1, 1965
Monumental Sculpture and Decorative
Art: XIIth–XVth Century
h

1964 – 65
Several small exhibits in connection
with Fine Arts and German classes,
including Dürer prints★
h

October 8 – November 7, 1965
Paul Klee: Graphic Work – Seventy
Etchings and Lithographs
org: Museum of Modern Art, New
York

April 18 – May 14, 1966
Eight Young German Painters: Antes,
Gembe, Bohrmann, Croissant,
Dahmen, Hoehme, Micel, Reuter
c, org: National Carl Schurz
Association, Philadelphia, and Gunter
Franke Gallery

May 21 – June 14, 1966
Spirit as Form: The Embodiment of the
Awesome in Primitive and
Contemporary Sculpture
c, org: Harvard Museum Training
Course students

November 1 – December 10, 1966
Bauhaus Faculty: Albers, Bayer, Bill,
Feininger, Itten, Kandinsky, Klee,

Marcks, Moholy-Nagy, Muche,
Schlemmer, Stoelzl
c

February 13 – April 1, 1967
Art of the Northern Renaissance

October 1967
Modern German Art: Works from the
Permanent Collection
h

October 16 – November 25, 1967
German Expressionism and Abstract
Art: A Decade of Collecting
h

November 28 – December 27, 1967
Graphic Art of Albrecht Dürer
h

January 11 – February 10, 1968
Giorgio Morandi: A Retrospective
c, org: Harvard Museum Training
Course students

February 26 – March 30, 1968
European Sources of German Baroque
Art
h

April 15 – May 11, 1968
Max Ernst: Works on Paper
org: Museum of Modern Art, New
York

October 26 – November 29, 1968
From Romanticism to Realism: Aspects
of German Nineteenth Century Art
h

December 11, 1968 – February 8, 1969
Renaissance and Reformation: German
Prints of the Sixteenth Century
h

February 18 – March 29, 1969
Art of the 20th Century, I:
Expressionism
h

April 9 – May 31, 1969
Art of the 20th Century, II:
Constructivism, Suprematism, Abstract
Art
h

January 7 – February 21, 1970
Dürer and Brueghel: A Century of
Humanism
h

March 5 – April 18, 1970
The Baroque Theatre
h

March 23 – April 13, 1970
The World of Charlemagne
org: German Center, Boston

April 15 – June 13, 1970
Jugendstil

June 18 – September 4, 1970
Dada 1916–1966: Documents of the
International Dada Movement
org: Hans Richter for the Goethe
Institute, Munich

November 3 – 28, 1970
Graphics 70: Germany
c, org: University of Kentucky

December 16, 1970 – February 13, 1971
Ernst Barlach (1870–1938)
c

March 4 – April 3, 1971
Auch Kleine Dinge: Dürer and the
Decorative Tradition
c, h

April 30 – September 3, 1971
Concepts of the Bauhaus: The Busch-
Reisinger Collection
c, h

July 12 – August 28, 1971
Painted Postcards and Letters from the
Collection of the Altonaer Museum in

Hamburg
c, org: Altonaer Museum, Hamburg

October 21 – November,* 1971
The Sculpture of Franz Barwig
c, org: Austrian Institute

November 4 – December 4, 1971
The World between the Ox and the
Swine
org: Rhode Island School of Design,
Providence

December 15 – January 22, 1971
A Glove and other Images of Reverie
and Apprehension: the Graphic Suites
of Max Klinger
c, org: International Exhibitions
Foundation

February 2 – 28, 1972
Five Hundred Years of Wine in the
Arts
c, org: Fromm and Sichel, Inc., San
Francisco

March 21 – April 29, 1972
Erich Heckel: Watercolors, Drawings
and Graphics
org: Winnipeg Art Gallery and Brücke
Museum

May 11 – June 24, 1972
Arnulf Rainer
org: Austrian Federal Ministry of
Education

May 1972
A Tribute to Venice

October 5 – November 18, 1972
German Master Drawings of the
Nineteenth Century
c, t, Metropolitan Museum, New York;
National Gallery of Canada, Ottowa;
Minneapolis Institute of Arts

December 1972 – January 16, 1973
Humanism in the North
h

January 22 – February 28, 1973
Peter Ackermann and Herman
Waldenburg: Graphic Works by Two
Berlin Artists
org: Goethe Institute Boston

February 6 – March 3, 1973
Selections from the Edith Gregor
Halpert Collection
org: Institute of Contemporary Art,
Boston

March 10 – April 7, 1973
Drawings by Jan Groth
org: Steingrim Laursen*

May 2 – June 23, 1973
Ferdinand Hodler
c, t, University Museum, Berkeley,
Calif., and Solomon R. Guggenheim
Museum, New York

Summer 1973
German Art of the 20th Century
h

September 19 – October 11, 1973
Margaret Fisher: Drawing, Watercolors,
Gouaches
c

November 2 – December 15, 1973
Ernst Matthes (1878–1918)

November 10, 1973 – January 1974
Exhibitions for Fine Arts Classes
h

November 30, 1973 – January 5, 1974
George Kolbe [with] Sculpture from
the Collection of B. Gerald Cantor
c, org: Johnson Museum, Cornell
University, Ithaca, N.Y.

January 6 – 23, 1974
Dürer Prints from the Collection of the
Fogg Museum
h

February 2 – March 9, 1974
Three Swiss Painters: Cuno Amiet,
Giovanni Giacometti, Augusto
Giacometti

April – May 1974
Teaching Exhibit for Humanities 127:
20th c. German and Austrian works
h

April* – June 17, 1974
Theatrical Drawings and Watercolors
by George Grosz
c, t, Benton Museum, University of
Connecticut; Galerie Nationale du
Canada; Krannert Art Museum,
University of Illinois; State University
of New York, Purchase; Wichita Art
Museum

June – August, 1974
German Expressionist Paintings from
the Permanent Collection
h

Summer 1974
Josef and Anni Albers and their Students
from Black Mountain College
h

October 18 – November 9, 1974
The World of the Late Middle Ages in
the Diebold Schilling Chronicle (1507–
1513)
c, org: CIBA-Geigy Corp.

January – March 1975
Craft into Art: 1880–1950
h

March 15 – April 26, 1975
Eucharistic Vessels of the Middle Ages
c, org: Cleveland Art Museum

May 2 – 19, 1975
Teaching Exhibition for Humanities
120 (Dürer, Cranach, Baldung,
Burgkmair)
h

April 29 – May 17, 1975
Calligraphy by Neugebauer
c

May 21 – June 28, 1975
Expressionist Prints of the 20th Century
h

July 16 – August 30, 1975
New European Graphics
h

October 15 – December 3, 1975
Max Ernst: Works from the Menil
Family Collection
c, org: DeMenil Family and Institute for
the Arts, Rice University, Houston

November 7 – 17, 1975
Works in conjunction with Fine Arts 13
h

November 7 – January 17, 1976
Cookie Molds from 17th to 19th
Century Europe
c, Goethe Institute and Busch-Reisinger

December 16 – January 17, 1976
Klee and Kandinsky
h

February 4 – March 4, 1976
Romanticism in the Graphic Arts
h

February 23 – March 17, 1976
Works by Emil Nolde
h

March 13 – April 17, 1976
Formulation: Articulation – Selected
Prints of Josef Albers
h

May 7 – June 19, 1976*
Works by A. Giacometti, Menzel,
Hodler, Klee, Arp
h

July – August 1976
19th and 20th century German prints
and drawings★
h

November 9 – 27, 1976
Color of the Middle Ages
c, org: University of Pittsburgh

December 7, 1976 – January 3, 1977
Graphic Art in Germany Today
c, org: Deutsche Lufthansa and Goethe
Institute

February 23 – May 7, 1977
German and Netherlandish Art of the
Period of Dürer and Breughel
h

May 24 – July 15, 1977
The D. Thomas Bergen Collection of
German Expressionist Drawings
c

July 28 – September 17, 1977
Max Beckmann Prints
org: Goethe Institute, supplemented by
h

October 12 – November 21, 1977
European Graphic Romantic Art
h

November 28, 1977 – January 21, 1978
From Menzel to Moholy-Nagy: Works
on Paper
h

February 10 – April 5, 1978
Paul Klee
h

March 6 – April, 1978
Käthe Kollwitz: Sculpture and Graphic
Works
c, org: Goethe Institute Boston

April 25 – June 10, 1978
Medieval Stained Glass from New
England

c, org: Tufts Fine Arts Students
Exhibition, Tufts University, Medford,
Mass.

June 12 – August 11, 1978
Paintings by Hannes Beckmann
c, org: Goethe Institute

June 27 – July 28, 1978
Contemporary Austrian Painting and
Prints
c, org: Vienna Central Savings Bank
and Austrian Consul, Boston

September 6 – October 21, 1978
Adolf Wölfli: A Retrospective
c, org: Wölfli Foundation, Bern Art
Museum

**December 6, 1978 – January 17,
1979**
Wassily Kandinsky/Constructivist Art/
75 Years of Collecting at the Busch-
Reisinger Museum
h

January 24 – February 28, 1979
19th Century German Romantics
h

January 14 – March 1, 1979
Works from the Permanent Collection:
Drawings and Prints from Central
Europe, 1870–1933
h

Spring 1979
The Our Father series by Max
Pechstein

March 12 – May 12, 1979
Anders Zorn: Etchings

June 1979
Works from the Collections in Honor
of Helmut Schmidt's Visit
h

September 12 – October 20, 1979
Conrad Felixmüller: Graphic Works

c, org: University of Virginia Art
Museum, Charlottesville

April 10 – May 2, 1980
The Soliloquy and the Perfect Kiss –
James Lee Byars

March 12 – May 4, 1980
From David to Courbet: Graphic works
h

March 12 – April 26, 1980
From Werkbund to Bauhaus: Art and
Design in Germany 1900–1934
h

May 9 – June 25, 1980
Horst Jannsen: Master Drawings
c, org: International Exhibitions
Foundation

Summer 1980
19th and 20th Century Paintings and
Sculptures/Prints and Drawings by
Ernst Barlach
h

September 25 – November 8, 1980
Gabriele Münter: From Munich to
Murnau
c, t, Princeton Art Museum

November 21, 1980 – January 17, 1981
Klee and Kandinsky: Works from the
Harvard Collections and the Solomon
R. Guggenheim Museum
h

February 27 – April 13, 1981
German Art of the Twenties
h

April 16 – May 6, 1981
Twentieth Century Abstract Art
h

May 19 – June 27, 1981
From Impressionism to the Bauhaus:

German Master Prints from the Harvard
Collections
h

July 5 – August 28, 1981
19th Century German Drawings and
Watercolors
h

September 7 – November 11, 1981
20th Century Works on Paper from the
Permanent Collection
h

October 28 – December 22, 1981
From Mengs to Menzel: Nineteenth
Century German Drawings
h

November 7, 1981 – January 9, 1982
The Graphic Works of Max Klinger
c, org: Institute für Auslandsbeziehung,
Stuttgart, and Goethe Institute, Boston

February 8 – March 24, 1982
19th and 20th Century Works from the
Permanent Collection
h

February – March 1982
American Paintings from the Fogg Art
Museum Collection I
h

March 1982
Manuscripts by Heinrich Heine
h

March 23 – August 25, 1982
American Paintings from the Fogg Art
Museum Collection II
h

April 5 – May 22, 1982
Art of the Weimar Era
h

June 7 – October 30, 1982
Bauhaus Art and Design
h

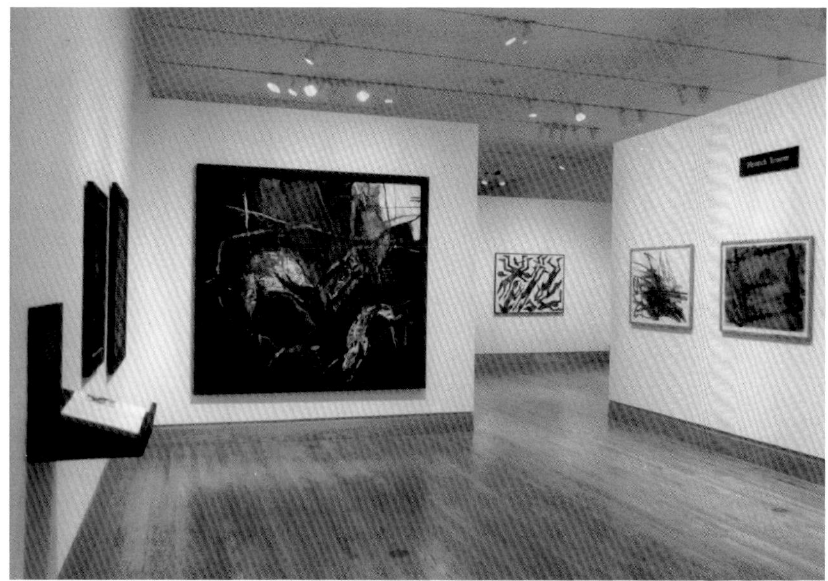

Installation view of Twelve Artists from the German Democratic Republic, 1989

November 8 – December 31, 1982
German Art of the Latter 19th Century

November 8 – December 31, 1982
Berlin: Images of the City in Graphic
Art
h

**January 31 – March 5 and July 8 –
August 26, 1983**
Prints by Ernst Barlach
h

**January 31 – March 5 and July 5 –
August 26, 1983**
Aspects of Jugenstil
h

March 14 – April 29, 1983
From the Realists to the Expressionists:
works on paper by Central European
Artists from 1870 to 1918
h

May 10 – July 1, 1983
A Tribute to Walter Gropius
h

September 1 – October 9, 1983
19th century drawings from the
Permanent Collection
h

October 6 – November 27, 1983
Edvard Munch: Master Printmaker –
Prints from the Philip and Lynn Straus
Collection
c, t, Neuberger Museum at State
University of New York

October 18 – December 11, 1983
Rembrandt: A Selection of His Works
h

December 29 – February 19, 1984
German Painting 1760–1960: A New
Installation
h

February 28 – April 8, 1984
Northern Renaissance Art: Selected
Works
h

April 17 – June 17, 1984
Joseph Beuys Drawings
c, org: Anthony D'Offay, London

June 26 – August 19, 1984
One Hundred Caricatures from
Simplicissimus
c, org: Goethe Institute, Munich

July 1984 – June 1985
German Sculpture, 1500–1960: A New
Installation
h

June 22 – September 15, 1985
Masterpieces of European Art
h

September 26 – November 10, 1985
The Architecture of Walter Gropius
c, t, Bauhaus-Archiv, Berlin;
Architekturmuseum, Frankfurt

October 21, 1985 – January 5, 1986
Modern Art at Harvard
h

November 21, 1985 – January 12, 1986
Prints and Drawings from the Time of
Holbein and Brueghel
h

January 21 – March 10, 1986
German Sculpture from the Permanent
Collection
h

March 15 – May 18, 1986
The Age of Romanticism
h

May 22 – July 13, 1986
German Twentieth Century Works on
Paper
h

October 10 – November 30, 1986
Bauhaus Photography
c,
org: Institut für Auslandsbeziehungen,
Stuttgart

July 6 – September 28, 1986
German Realist Drawings of the 1920s

t, Solomon R. Guggenheim Museum,
New York; Staatsgalerie Stuttgart

Spring 1987
Sculpture from the Permanent
Collection
h

April 25 – June 14, 1987
Friedrich Weinbrenner, Architect of
Karlsruhe [last exhibit in Adolphus
Busch Hall]
c, org: University of Pennsylvania,
Philadelphia

September 26 – November 29, 1987
El Lissitzky 1890–1941
c, t, Sprengel Museum, Hanover,
Galerie Moritzburg, Halle

November 1987 – September 1989
Selections from the Collections of the
Busch-Reisinger Museum
h

September 16 – November 5, 1989
Twelve Artists from the German
Democratic Republic
c, t, Wight Art Gallery, UCLA;
University of Michigan Museum of Art,
Ann Arbor; Albuquerque Museum

January 20 – March 18, 1990
Envisioning America: Prints, Drawings
and Photographs by George Grosz and
His Contemporaries
c, t, Robert Gore Rifkind Center at Los
Angeles County Museum of Art

May 26 – June 2, 1990
The Fredric Wertham Collection
c, h

April 27 – June 23, 1991
Adolph Menzel 1815–1905: Master
Drawings from Berlin
c, org: Art Services International,
Alexandria, Va.

FURTHER READING

General

The Busch-Reisinger Museum, Harvard University. New York: Abbeville Press, 1980. Highlights of the collection, including related works from the Fogg.

Germanic Museum Bulletin, Cambridge, six issues, 1935–38.

Haxthausen, Charles W. "The Busch-Reisinger Museum, Harvard: The Germanic Tradition." *Apollo* (May 1978): 52–59. Highlights of the collection.

Jones, Caroline A. *Modern Art at Harvard*. New York: Abbeville Press, 1985. Chapter on Charles Kuhn and his acquisitions of modern art, in the context of the Fogg's activities.

Mortimer, Kristin A., with contributions by William G. Klingelhofer. *Harvard University Art Museums: A Guide to the Collections*. Cambridge, Mass.: Harvard University Art Museums; New York: Abbeville Press, 1985. Section on Busch-Reisinger collection.

History and Policy

Annual Reports to the President of Harvard University on the Germanic Museum and Busch-Reisinger Museum, 1903–present.

"The Germanic Museum: Dedicatory Exercises in New Lecture Hall — The Addresses." *The Harvard Bulletin* 6, no. 7 (Nov. 18, 1903).

Francke, Kuno. "Deutsche Kultur in den Vereinigten Staaten und das Germanische Institut der Harvard-University." *Deutsche Rundschau*, Bd. 111, Berlin 1902.

———. "Ein künstlerisches Kartell mit Amerika." *Internationale Wochenschrift für Wissenschaft Kunst und Technik* (May 30, 1908): 673–77.

———. "Die Aufgaben und Ziele des Germanischen Museums der Harvard Universität." *Internationale Wochenschrift für Wissenschaft Kunst und Technik.* (August 15, 1908): 1033–44.

———. "Emperor William's Gifts to Harvard University." *International Studio* 36, no. 141 (November, 1908): 13–18.

———. *Deutsche Arbeit in Amerika,* Leipzig: Felix Meiner Verlag, 1930.

Goldman, Guido. *A History of the Germanic Museum at Harvard University.* Cambridge, Mass.: The Minda de Gunzburg Center for European Studies, Harvard University, 1989.

Kuhn, Charles L. "The New Policy of the Germanic Museum." *Harvard Alumni Bulletin* (February 19, 1932): 610–12.

Pommerin, Reiner. "Die Gründung des Germanischen Museums an der Harvard Universität. Zur Geschichte deutscher Kulturpolitik in den USA unter Kaiser Wilhelm II." *Archiv für Kulturgeschichte,* 61. Band 1979 Heft 2, S. 420–30.

von Ungern-Sternberg, Franziska. *Die Gründung des Germanischen Museums in Cambridge, Massachusetts. Kulturpolitische Hintergründe für ihre Realisierung.* M.A. Thesis, Hamburg University, 1990.

Descriptions, Catalogues, and Checklists

Bowron, Edgar Peters. *European Paintings before 1900 in the Fogg Art Museum: A Summary Catalogue Including Paintings in the Busch-Reisinger Museum.* Cambridge, Mass.: Harvard University Art Museums, 1990. Includes forty-three paintings from the Busch-Reisinger collection.

Deutsche Kunst des 20. Jahrhunderts aus dem Busch-Reisinger Museum, Harvard University, Cambridge, USA. Frankfurt: Städtische Galerie im Städelschen Kunstinstitut, 1982. Exhibition catalogue, edited by C.W. Haxthausen, with essays on various parts of the twentieth-century collection.

Farmer, John David, ed. *Concepts of the Bauhaus: The Busch-Reisinger Museum Collection,* 1971. Exhibition catalogue and complete list of Bauhaus holdings.

Francke, Kuno. *Handbook of the Germanic Museum.* Cambridge, seven editions, 1906–29. Description of the reproductions installed, first in Rogers Hall and then in Adolphus Busch Hall.

Kuhn, Charles L. "Barlach and Kolbe in the Germanic Museum." *Fogg Museum Bulletin* 3, no. 1 (November 1933): 8–12; reprinted in *The American-German Review* 2, no. 2 (1936).

———. "Eine fränkische Madonna des frühen 15 Jahrhunderts" (with English trans.). *Pantheon* 19 (May 1937): 142–43, sup 18.

———. "Blair Madonna, Franconian, about 1420." *Germanic Museum Bulletin* 1, no. 5 (1937): 31–34.

———. "German Art of the Eighteenth Century." *Germanic Museum Bulletin* 1, no. 2 (1936): 7–12.

———. "America and the Bauhaus." *The American-German Review* 15, no. 2 (December 1948): 16–22.

———. "Recent Acquisitions. The Busch-Reisinger Museum." *The American-German Review* 19, no. 2 (December 1952): 14–21.

———. "Unknown Relief by Peter Flötner." *Art Quarterly* 17, no. 2 (1954): 108–15.

———. "The Busch-Reisinger Museum: Three Years of Collecting." *The American-German Review* 22, no. 6 (August–September 1956): 19–23.

———. *German Expressionism and Abstract Art: The Harvard Collections.* Cambridge, Mass.: Harvard University Press, 1957. Supplemental volume published by Harvard University Press in 1967.

———. *German and Netherlandish Sculpture 1280–1800: The Harvard Collections.* Cambridge, Mass.: Harvard University Press, 1965.

———. "Riemenschneider in the Harvard Collections." *Art Bulletin* 56, no. 2 (June 1974): 244–47.

———. "Mairhauser Epitaph: An Example of Late Sixteenth-Century Lutheran Iconography." *Art Bulletin* 58, no. 4 (December 1976): 542–46.

Nerdinger, Winfried. *The Architect Walter Gropius: Drawings, Prints and Photographs from the Busch-Reisinger Museum, Harvard University, and from the Bauhaus-Archiv Berlin, with Complete Project Catalogue.* Berlin: Gebr. Mann Verlag, 1985. Exhibition catalogue with additional information on the Walter Gropius Archive.

———, ed. *The Walter Gropius Archive: An Illustrated Catalogue of the Drawings, Prints and Photographs in the Walter Gropius Archive at the Busch-Reisinger Museum,*

Harvard University. New York: Garland Publishing, 1990. 3 vols. Illustrations of all the drawings in the Gropius Archive along with reproductions of many prints and photographs.

Verzeichnis der galvanischen Nachbildungen deutschen Silbergerätes gestiftet aus freiwilligen Beiträgen dem Germanischen Museum des Harvard-College. Berlin: W. Büxenstein, 1903. Catalogue of the electrotype reproductions of German metalwork donated by Berlin citizens in 1903.

The Fredric Wertham Collection, Gift of his wife Hesketh, Cambridge, Mass.: Busch-Reisinger Museum, 1990. Exhibition catalogue with essays on the collector and an annotated checklist of the complete bequest.

Buildings

Francke, Kuno. "The Germanic Museum of Harvard." *Art and Archaeology* 28, no. 6 (December, 1929): 233–39.

The New Building for the Busch-Reisinger Museum. The Design for Werner Otto Hall by Gwathmey Siegel & Associates. Cambridge, Mass.: Busch-Reisinger Museum, 1989. Illustrates plans, elevations, perspectives, and sections, with texts by the architect and museum representatives.

ACKNOWLEDGMENTS

Our gratitude is extended to the European Friends of the Busch-Reisinger Museum for support of this volume.

Annette Schlagenhauff, the 1990–91 intern at the Busch-Reisinger Museum funded by the National Endowment for the Arts, has ably assisted with preparation, especially the section on eighteenth-century porcelains. Elizabeth Gombosi, Michael Nedzweski, and Rick Stafford of the Photograph Services Department have been most accommodating and resourceful in providing the images in the book. Peter Walsh has carefully supervised production; Evelyn Rosenthal, the project editor, expertly worked on copy and layout, and Becky Hunt proofread the manuscript. The volume was sensitively designed by Eleanor Bradshaw of Portsmouth, N.H.

Our thanks to the following for permission to publish: Harvard University Archives, Harley Holden, curator, for quotations from the Bestelmeyer correspondence in the collected papers of A. Lawrence Lowell; and the Architekturmuseum Technische Universitat München for the Bestelmeyer section drawing of Adolphus Busch Hall (p.36). Our thanks as well to Otto-Versand, Hamburg, for the photograph of Werner Otto (p. 17); Lubosh Cech, for the *Twelve Artists from the German Democratic Republic* installation photo (p.118); Gwathmey Siegel & Associates for the architectural drawings of Werner Otto Hall (pp. 38 and 39); Christopher S. Johnson for the photo of the completed building (p. 40); and the Herald-Traveler archive at the Boston University School of Communications for the 1903 clipping with A. Howard Walker's rendering of the museum (p. 34).